Coaching the Serenity Prayer Lifestyle

Coaching the Serenity Prayer Lifestyle

How to Accept What You Cannot
Change and Change
What You Can

Dan C. Crenshaw

To order additional copies of this book, contact:
Xlibris Corporation
1-888-795-4274
www.Xlibris.com
Orders@Xlibris.com
63985

CONTENTS

Introduction...9

Part 1

The Serenity Prayer: A Coach for Purposeful Living

1 The Serenity Prayer—A Lifestyle with Endless Applications............15
2 The Serenity Prayer: Recovery and Discovery.................................30

Part 2

The Serenity Prayer: A Coach for Healthy Family Living

3 Taming Control/Change Issues in Marriage 47
4 Teenagers: Harnessing Their Energies with Wisdom
and Courage..77
5 Stepping into Stepfamily Living with Wisdom 93

Part 3

The Serenity Prayer: A Coach for Healing Inner Turmoil

6 Healing Grief with Courage and Wisdom 111
7 Healing Trauma with Courage...130
8 Shortchanging Shame: Taming the Shaming Malaise.....................144

Part 4

The Serenity Prayer: A Coach for Healthy Relationships

9   Good Boundaries: Bound for the Promised Land...........................157
10 Responding to Difficult People with Serenity 173
11 Networking: Changing What You Thought
    You Could Not Change...188

Author's Note...197

Dedication

This book is dedicated to my identical twin brother, David. His newspaper articles served as an inspirational catalyst for me to embark upon a writing venture. My mind-set regarding my writing aptitude was transformed. What I previously thought was unchangeably cast in stone began to be sculptured into a writing gift. My disbelief turned into a conviction that my writing ability could be heightened.

As a result, I wrote articles for newspapers as well. As these one hundred articles took shape, they became sculptured stepping-stones to writing this book. I did not want to leave one stone unturned. Discovering my artistic gift of crafting impactful words became my passion.

With my experience and education in ministry, chaplaincy, and professional counseling, it was natural for me to gravitate toward writing this book on the Serenity Prayer. This book is also dedicated to that beautifully crafted prayer, which has profound meaning that cannot be fully expressed in words. The Serenity Prayer is to be experienced.

Introduction

God, give us grace to accept with serenity the things that cannot be changed, the courage to change the things that should be changed, and the wisdom to distinguish the one from the other. (Elisabeth Sifton, *The Serenity Prayer: Faith and Politics in Times of Peace and War,* W.W. Norton, October 2003, p. 277 quotes this version as the authentic original.*)*

Why has the Serenity Prayer become one of the three most well-known prayers in the world? The Serenity Prayer strikes a common chord. Accepting what we cannot change with serenity and changing what we can with courage is a universal yearning. As a result, this prayer has been translated into many languages and is used by millions of people.

One purpose of this book is to broaden the horizons for those of you who already are experiencing this prayer's remarkable benefits. This book will help you to experience the prayer in a much more purposeful and practical manner. The well-known prayer will become like a close spiritual coach deeply concerned about your well-being. The purpose of this prayer concerns coaching you to develop a lifestyle with healthy behaviors, thoughts, and feelings.

Pondering this prayer and writing this book has resulted in my experiencing the prayer afresh and anew. Now, when I say the Serenity Prayer, its personal impact is greater. It sinks more deeply into my soul and adds a greater purpose and direction to my life.

This book is also written to introduce the prayer to you newcomers as an additional enhancing spiritual resource. By reading this book, you can visit and revisit the Serenity Prayer until you no longer feel like a visitor. You will feel intimately at home with the prayer as you experience more personal spiritual privacy with God. As you live the Serenity Prayer lifestyle, you will become more peaceful. Your prayerful journey inward will radically affect your lifestyle regarding how you spiritually journey outward. God will become your ultimate coach as this prayer provides a channel in which to tap God's spiritual guidance.

It is natural for you to experience unchangeable circumstances that you would like to change. There is not a day that goes by that you do not encounter unchangeable undesirable situations. These events often result in internal strife. For example, these unalterable events may include exasperating occurrences such as a traffic jam. On the upper end of the spectrum, the situation may be a devastating tragedy. These scenarios unattended can block your view of the future. They can affect your life for a day or linger for a lifetime. They can diminish your feeling of the rich, peaceful, guiding presence of God. A sports coach will take a frustrated player to the side to provide a motivational presence to let go of the past and dive back into the game.

You also need to have the wisdom to know what you cannot change. It can be difficult to face the reality that some of your desires are not possible. Facing reality can leave you disturbed. This lack of peacefulness can result in your being greatly perturbed. A white flag may be the imagery that represents your defeated attitude.

On the other hand, accepting what you cannot change with serenity is an attitudinal and behavioral victory. You will be left with a sense of dignity that is full of energy. You will not retreat from life. Hope will reign as you venture toward your future possibilities. As optimism reigns, you will be alertly looking for aspects of life that you should change. You will be able to positively seize the moment, instead of feeling negatively besieged by unalterable circumstances. The prayerful coach says, "Charge toward your purpose in life."

It can be an enormous relief to remind yourself that you cannot control everything. You will not be wasting energy preoccupied about the past. Future concerns will not hold you in their grasp. While you will learn from the past and set goals for the future, your spiritual empowerment will result in living primarily in the present. Consequently, the past and the future will be supportive to your present Serenity Prayer lifestyle.

Not only does this prayer address what you cannot change, it also can help you focus your energies in making appropriate changes. You will know that just because a matter is changeable, it does not necessarily mean it is an appropriate goal. You may be barking up the wrong tree, stripping the tree of its protective bark. Appropriate changes can place the music of a singing lark in the heart of the tree of your life. You can become inspired by the song of living that the Serenity Prayer offers. You will not be inundated by the throng of distractions that can steer you wrong. The multitude of distractions can jam-up your life. Being coached by the Serenity Prayer can enable you to get out of the jam and move toward telling the distractions to scram.

Furthermore, the prayer infers that you need to change what you can in a positive manner. If you change what you should change in a detrimental manner, you may have been better-off if you did not become involved in the first place. If the end does not justify the means, the goal that you obtained may have been reached by being mean. How you journey is as important as your destination. Sportsmanlike conduct can increase the quality of your living in the game of life.

The Serenity Prayer also deals with the necessity to have the wisdom to distinguish between what is changeable and what is unchangeable. Learning to one's delight that what was previously thought to be unchangeable is in actuality changeable is a powerful enlightenment. This priceless attitudinal change is briefly personally illustrated in the dedication of this book. My twin brother's writing successes helped me believe that I could take my writing skills to another level.

In a nutshell, this prayer reminds you that if you remain chronically distressed about what you cannot change, you may feel like a nut living in a shell. What you cannot change can capture you and hold you captive. On the other hand, as you become captivated by the Serenity Prayer, you can be set free.

You can become a gracious host inviting the future to become your guest. By being hospitable toward the future, you can provide hospitality to all the opportunities at present that grace your place. As a result, the attitudes that you have, the behaviors that you demonstrate, and your emotional state are all at stake.

Accordingly, your whole demeanor and lifestyle depend upon how effectively you handle unchangeable and changeable matters. The legacy that you leave and your life's footprints are connected to the dynamics of this impactful prayer. For this reason, this is perhaps the most universally well-known prayer.

You have experienced events from which you need to recover. By impacting your behaviors, feelings, and thoughts, this masterful prayer's meaning and application can positively empower your recoveries. This book specifically applies this prayer to nine common life challenges listed in the table of contents.

Enough of these issues apply to your life to enable you to learn how to apply the prayer to all aspects of your daily living. Therefore, providing a resourceful coach to enable you to utilize this prayer as a lifestyle is the main purpose of this book. Reading this book can become a significant help. Experiencing this book is paramount. The introduction and the first two chapters are foundational for the application of the prayer. May the content of this book grant you a lifestyle that flows forward like a sparkling brook.

To more serene living,

Dan C. Crenshaw

Part 1

The Serenity Prayer:
A Coach for Purposeful Living

Chapter 1

The Serenity Prayer
—A Lifestyle with Endless Applications

God, give us grace to accept with serenity the things that cannot be changed, courage to change the things that should be changed, and the wisdom to distinguish the one from the other. (Elisabeth Sifton, *The Serenity Prayer: Faith and Politics in Times of Peace and War,* W.W. Norton October 2003, p. 277 *quotes this version as the authentic original.)*

The Serenity Prayer can give you meaning and purpose
That can enable you to live life overflowing with a peaceful surplus.

Not only can it become the lifeblood to help sustain effective living,
The Serenity Prayer can enable you to have wisdom in giving.

Deciding that you deserve to become more serene is foundational in gaining a more gratifying life. Instead of sabotaging inner peace, you can enhance more tranquil living. You will become more open to personally explore and apply the Serenity Prayer to important matters of daily living.

What a purposeful, peaceful heart you would have if you gazed at life through the eyes of the magnificent Serenity Prayer! Your eyes would twinkle like the stars in the night. With a tranquil glow, you would brighten the lives of those you touch. Serenity, wisdom, and courage would come together in concert producing a sterling live symphonic harmony. These three virtues would serve as a foundational tripod triumphantly supporting a harmonious music in your life. Harmony in your behaviors, thoughts, and feelings would result as this prayer orchestrates your life to be in tune spiritually.

As a result, this prayer can become the tuning fork to keep your lifestyle in tune with a wise, purposeful living. The tuning fork can enable you to make wise decisions regarding your future forks on the road. As a result, the prayerful tuning fork will create a melodious tone in your life.

This book also quarries beneath the surface of the prayer as there are many golden thoughts that can be mined. These prayerful ideas can saturate your mind. You will not mind incorporating this prayer as the mainstay of your life. As a result, you can become increasingly mindful of its unlimited personal applications.

The Serenity Prayer will become like a lighthouse—a beacon leading the ship of your life toward its destination. Your life's ship will not become mired in shallow waters or smashed against jagged rocks. The Serenity Prayer then will instill within you a sense of safety and security. It can become a welcoming beacon beckoning you to live your life in a purposeful direction. Then, with this clear direction, you can avert a way of destruction, resulting in escaping avoidable disruptions. Prayerfully finding your purpose can frame your life. As a result, the prayer can become your framework for living. You will not feel like you have been framed or maimed by life; the prayer provides thoughts, feelings to enable you to move through the strife.

This extraordinary prayer was used in a sermon preached by Reinhold Neihbor during World War II. When our world was out of control, thousands of copies were passed to soldiers. They were struggling to gain some measure of serenity in the midst of a catastrophic war. This prayer can also be personally applied to the complexities of our modern world. As a result, this prayer can become a balm in the midst of life's exploding bombs. The Serenity Prayer can move you forward in any kind of recovery as it channels wisdom and courage—which is a priceless discovery. *When hope is waning and your life is beginning to languish, this prayer can grant you peace and lessen your anguish.*

Since Alcoholics Anonymous (AA) emphasizes change and acceptance matters, this amazing prayer was a natural match for the spiritual part of this recovery program. A significant statement of AA is "Let go and let God." This statement emphasizes accepting what we cannot change with serenity. Letting go and letting God can help bring serenity in the midst of uncontrollable events.

Perhaps our greatest challenge then is to let go and accept the unchangeable aspects of life. By letting these unchangeable matters of life go, God can lead you to other challenges that you can change. As a result, this prayer can help you to have a balance between acceptance and change—letting go of what you cannot change and changing what you can. You will know when to stop and when to go.

> It is very difficult to "let go" of the unalterable matters of life.
> These challenges can become an altar call when you falter in reducing
> your internal strife.

The second jewel in this prayer, changing what you can, provides wisdom to enlighten your paths. You can be reminded that you can become a positive change agent regarding yourself, your circumstances, and the world at large. You can have the courage and wisdom to change what needs to be changed. It takes wisdom to discern what you need to accomplish and courage to step up to the plate and meet the challenge. Without *wisdom*, you will not be competent to change what you should change. Lacking *serenity*, you may become overly frustrated when obstacles come your way. Missing *courage*, *you* may not have the fortitude to take the risk to follow through. A good coach provides wisdom, inspires courage, and gives stability through deep, abiding serenity.

Steven Lane Taylor's delightful book *Row, Row, Row Your Boat: A Guide for Living Life in the Divine Flow* strikes the heart, soul, and spirit of the Serenity Prayer. Putting your faith in the divine flow is the hallmark of the Serenity Prayer. The divine flow leads you to change what you can. The stream is the underlying divine, supportive current helping you to flow gently down the stream, making the change possible. As a result, this marvelous book brings the principles of the Serenity Prayer in full focus. In effect, the splendid book orchestrates how you can allow God to grant you the serenity to accept what you cannot change, the courage to change what you should change, and the wisdom to know the difference. The divine flow, in its own creative fashion, can become a lifelong coach providing guiding principles to live the Serenity Prayer lifestyle. Your life can certainly flow more gently down the stream when you have the serenity to accept what you cannot change, the courage to change what you should change, and the wisdom to know the difference. (Brown Books Publishing Group, 2006)

Several years ago, I was director of a counseling center that was a satellite office of a hospital's counseling department. Because of a financial crisis, I was a part of a massive employee layoff. My career thereafter was not as fulfilling. Life began to flow when I let go of what I could not change. Then I became engrossed in writing. My first venture involved being accepted to write weekly articles for three newspapers. The first article that I wrote flowed with exciting ease. This experience helped me realize how much I enjoyed writing. My next venture involved writing this book. Accepting what I could not change led me to a next career passion. Writing this book flowed creatively, and I felt the undercurrent of the stream of God.

Wisdom to distinguish what was changeable from what was not, prevented me from tying my gift for writing in a knot. I began to experience the divine flow, and it flowed gently down the stream.

Therefore, my zeal for writing would not have been discovered if I was preoccupied with what I could not change. This prayer, then, can help you accept what you want to change but can't, without blaring out a rave and a rant. Then you can have the energy to change what you can and experience the momentum of moving toward your promised land.

As a result, the Serenity Prayer can help you move with and not against the grain of life. By allowing yourself to flow with life's grain, this prayer will become ingrained in your being. Your life will become astonishingly compelling as wisdom, courage, and serenity are increasingly indwelling. Serenity can grant you the calmness and patience to let go and let God. Courage can provide you the will to risk and branch out from your comfort zone. Wisdom can provide you with guidance. Then, your life will result in growing, glowing, and "flowing" with internal guiding light. The guidance will enable you to have a lifestyle that is right.

With the Serenity Prayer, you may take dead aim in reaching your goals. Composed concentration can bring your dreams to life. This classical prayer can be inspirational in helping you to step up to the plate and hit the ball in fair territory. You will not be as apt to run afoul.

When I was a senior in high school, I played on the golf team. On one occasion, we played a school much larger than ours. We were severe underdogs. I had my greatest round of golf in competition. I was addressing a thirty-five-foot putt at the final eighteenth hole that curled severely to the right. As I was preparing to putt, I overheard the opposing coach say, "If Dan sinks that putt, we will lose by one point." A sense of calm came over me. I stroked the putt, allowing for much break to the right. The speed and line were perfect, and it rolled into the center of the cup. We won 20-19. I shot a 74 on a very difficult course.

Golf as a game taught me much about the game of life. Being serene did not guarantee that I would have sunk the putt. It is clear that if I had been overly nervous, I could not have possibly given the ball the smooth stroke that it needed to reach its intended destination. Serene living helps us to tap into our greatest potential. Being at peace will prevent your negative thoughts from being torrential. Positive thoughts, with the mind at rest, can aid you to "row" toward your goals with direction and zest.

You can easily become preoccupied with something with which you have no control. You may become helpless, hapless, and possibly hopeless as you chase rabbits that you should let go. Your mind may be racing, spinning wheels, going nowhere.

When I was a child, I watched my neighbor cut a chicken's head off in preparation for the family meal. After the head was off, the chicken ran around in circles many times. With your head not working, you may head in the wrong direction. You may run in circles accomplishing little. With an unquiet mind, your life might be like a running sore. With a quiet mind, your life will likely soar. A quiet mind lives in the present, resulting in life becoming very pleasant. The Serenity Prayer, then, can help you to be engrossed in constructive life-changing efforts. As a result of becoming a positive change agent, your life will become more vibrant and purposeful.

Wisdom can magnify the power of this prayerful craft and enable you to become a crafty change agent. Serenity, in concert with wisdom and courage, can create a symphony. This beautiful music can produce an epiphany.

> *When you change matters in the wrong manner, there is no serenity.*
> *There will likely only be enmity.*

Then, how can you become a more effective change agent? You need wisdom, which is birthed out of tranquility. Your mind will be able to stay composed and focused. You can think more clearly. With flooding anxiety, you may be driven to distraction and not see the task at hand. Courage can grant you the will to follow through, and your lifestyle can come in handy.

Also, with flooding anxiety, your goals may drown as you go down for the third time. As a result, not obtaining your aspiration's goal may feel like a crime. Wrapping your arms around this prayer can be a life preserver keeping your goals from becoming dead in the water. The Serenity Prayer can help you toward your goals by inspiring you not to falter.

It is appropriate, then, that this prayer is called the Serenity Prayer because you have no foundation for courage or wisdom without being at ease. Staying unruffled makes life flow easier. The attitude of "easy does it" keeps a reserve of energy to preserve serenity. If you are trying too hard with an exorbitant amount of stress, it may be a signal to stop, look, and listen before your life becomes a mess. Then you can envision your mission more clearly and move toward your goal more sincerely, making the correct decision.

Then these traits of serenity, wisdom, and courage can prevent you from becoming a traitor sabotaging yourself. You will become loyal and faithful to your faith in God and your faith in yourself. Consequently, you will not become derailed as life rails away with a torrent of challenging situations. These three virtues will serve as buffers to avert being buffeted by the undercurrents of life. The windmill of support will empower you toward a powerful pilgrimage. Being coached can help keep the wind at your back, keeping your mission from being susceptible to crack.

Then you can become intentional and proactive in gaining a locus of control. As a result, you will not be infected by swarming destructive locusts that could eat away at your soul. You can become inspired to recover from the difficult unexpected bounces of the ball of life.

Next are thoughts on serenity, wisdom, and courage. These virtues can create the vibes to vibrate and invigorate your soul. By having this frame of mind, you can frame serenity, wisdom, and courage in the picture of your life. As you step out of the picture into the realm of life, serenity, wisdom, and courage can become your life's framework.

Think on these thoughts as you embark upon personally applying this prayer to the nuts and bolts of your life:

Serene Thoughts

To be with serenity is to be like a ship coming into its harbor to dock.
To be with serenity is to be like having character that is as solid as a rock.
To be serene is to be like a sparkling new ship set free at sea.
To gain serenity is to be like a soul experiencing eternity.

It is important to find your own unique repertoire regarding enhancing a sense of tranquility. For example, your thoughts can have a calming, relaxing effect. Ponder these thoughts in putting together your unique, peaceful inducing portfolio.

Contemplate a fresh stream
Reflecting the rays of a sunbeam.
Envision being splashed all over by a waterfall
Breathtakingly giving you a comforting shawl.

Envision a meadow full of flowers
And how you would feel lying there for hours.
Envision a mountain that is majestic and strong
With a calm lake reflecting its beauty all day long

Envision a white sandy seashore with beautiful sand dunes
And the sound of the waves playing relaxing tunes.
The ocean absorbs all attention, leaving your soul at rest
Resulting in you feeling your very best.

Envision a rose garden in full bloom.
You will be relaxed very soon.
Every color of roses that you can think of is there.
You are in the garden, and roses are everywhere.

The sweet smell of the roses radiates a savoring scent.
You are enraptured as your five senses are without a dent.
This experience has made your soul serene.
You have gained a glimpse of what true serenity can bring.

Allow your mind to go to your special, peaceful place.
Give your mind, body, and spirit a respite of grace.
The special qualities of this scene are beyond any word.
This serene place is more pleasant than the song of a blue bird.
Other sounds that are calming to you are delightfully heard.

The following is an example of going to a favorite place that I have written.

A Serene Beach Scene

You are walking down a comforting white sandy seashore. You feel the wonderful warm grains of sand between your toes. The warmth of the sand travels up your body and warms your heart, mind, and soul. A sense of well-being unfolds, and you begin to forget your woes. Your mind is becoming quietly alert, preparing you to live life alertly on your toes.

Ahead you see a magnificent grassy sandy sand dune. You use this nature's pillow to change your life's tune. You feel the warmth of the sand on your neck, coming through the grass. All of the worries are draining from your mind. Your tension is draining out of your body down through your feet into the sand. Your peaceful heart radiates a powerful glow. This sand dune is preparing your lifestyle to be in tune.

Next, you look up and see seagulls lazily flying across the sky. They seem to be in no hurry. They are flying effortlessly with the wind supporting their wings. There is an occasional flap of their wings. You are peaceful in the midst of the flaps of your life. The seagulls are flying in formation. Then you notice that they changed their normal flight position. They begin to form the letters of your name across the sky. You feel welcomed to this special place created just for you.

Then, you notice white puffy clouds. These clouds write your name in the sky. They affirm your sense of belonging. One cloud comes closer to you, beckoning you for a ride. You climb on the cloud and have an exhilarating experience. Lying on your back and floating across the sky brings a peaceful calmness. You are not experiencing a care in the world.

Presently you are back on the seashore. You notice the tide is rising, and the wave comes and brushes against your feet, giving you a powerful connection with the ocean. Then, your interest is piqued as you notice a figure of a person walking toward you.

You recognize a special calming inspirational person. It may be a spiritual figure, a historical figure, or a friend or relative of the past or present. Just being in this person's presence grants you a wonderful sense of safety and unconditional love. All the tension remaining in your body is draining away. This special place is your personal sanctuary. You find your soul at rest. Being coached can enable you to live at your best. You are ready to begin a more meaningful Serenity Prayer lifestyle quest.

You may adapt this scene and read it every day to heighten your quality of life. A sense of self-esteem, meaning, hope, empowerment, and purpose are its fruits. Calming thoughts grant you a gift of serenity. This soothing prayer can grant peacefulness that can last for an eternity.

As we consider a serene role model, Gandhi may come to mind. With a serene mind that birthed courage and wisdom, he became an astounding change agent. Thus, he had a huge impact with his peaceful nonviolent approach. He worked for civil rights from within. Also, he labored to free India from the tyranny of the British colonial authority.

Wisdom

Without wisdom is to be like a ship without a rudder. With insight, one can make healthy decisions without fear, which could make you shudder. When one's decisions are on shaky ground, it is hard for a positive benefit to be found. When one's decisions are sound, it makes your world sound more harmonious. Think about a prudent decision that you have made. Wisdom can be cultivated as the mind is serene. Good judgment can be activated by courage to help you to fulfill your dream.

As we think of a wise man, King Solomon may come to mind. He displayed enormous wisdom as a judge regarding two women who both claimed that a baby was theirs. One baby died in the night, and both women declared that the living infant was theirs. The king ordered one of his men to obtain a sword. Then he commanded that the child be cut in half and a portion be given to each woman.

The authentic mother pleaded for her child's life by asking that the infant be given to the other woman. Solomon then commanded that the child be given to this woman who demonstrated compassion for the infant. Through his wisdom, he set up a situation where the cream rose to the top. The bona fide mother surfaced. Then, the wisdom of Solomon began to spread throughout the land. (1 Kings 3:16-28)

Courage

With valor, one can carry out the changes that one needs to make. Courage is not the absence of fear. Courage uses wisdom to do what is right. Fear then loses its might. As a result, courage manages fear, steering us in the right direction.

Courage helps you to stare fear in the face and not blink. Then your valor can keep your eyes wide open, helping you to think. This concentration resulting in wisdom propels you to risk to experiencing some pain. This risk can change what you can, resulting in commendable gain. Heroic actions do not have to make headlines and ring bells. These behaviors of the valiant person speak for themselves.

President Roosevelt displayed courage during the Depression when he said, perhaps, his most famous words, "We have nothing to fear but fear itself." He provided great leadership during one of the most challenging times in the history of our country. *He stared fear in the face and did not blink. His hope for the future did not shrink.*

Serenity, wisdom, and courage in tandem then give you the emotional and spiritual stance to "flow" toward your potential. Your will becomes dynamically inclined as you stop placing energy on limitations and start placing vigor on your future possibilities.

Helping to Make This Book and This Prayer Become a More Powerful Coach

The following guiding questions are adapted to the nine different life challenges listed in the table of contents. These thought-provoking questions are placed at the end of each chapter to help you ponder the personal applications and implications of the Serenity Prayer. The resulting soul-searching enterprise can aid you in living the Serenity Prayer lifestyle as you apply this prayer to all aspects of your daily life. The questions are for you to revolutionize your behavior, thoughts, and feelings as you are guided into developing the Serenity Prayer lifestyle. They serve as coaches enabling you to dig deeply into your soul to help your life become more whole.

These questions embodied in the Serenity Prayer can then begin a personal lifelong quest in becoming more skillful in living the Serenity Prayer lifestyle. Then the Serenity Prayer can become increasingly embedded in your life. The prayer can help smooth out the edges of life and prevent your lifestyle from becoming coarse. The voice of your life will not become hoarse. The Serenity Prayer then is a great spiritual resource to help you keep the course.

The first two chapters are foundational for the more specific applications that are forthcoming.

Coaching Questions: Applying the Serenity Prayer in Your Daily Life

Remember:

Your life's efforts have not gone for naught. You can be commended for what you have already wrought. You are not starting from scratch. You have long since been hatched.

These questions and thoughts are for the purpose of serving as a personal coach. They can give you the opportunity to prayerfully discover solutions in your particular situation. You may discover an opportunity to build upon what you are already doing well and take another step forward. This exercise can become a profitable soul-searching pilgrimage.

1. **What unchangeable aspects of life do you need to accept?**

"Lord, help me to accept the aspects of my life that cannot be changed."
It is very difficult to let go of the unalterable aspects of life. They can bring us to the altar when we falter in reducing internal strife.

2. **What do you need to change that you can change regarding aspects of your life?**

"Lord, help me to change the things that I should change regarding the various aspects of my life."
We can make a difference that counts.

3. **What are some things that you may be striving to change in the wrong manner?**

"Lord, help me to change the things that I need to change in the right manner."

Does the end justify the means?

Is the process worthy of the progress?

Does the manner of change have good manners?

It can help by thinking of an example of what you have changed in a positive manner. Begin from a positive feeling.

When one changes things in the wrong way, there is no serenity.
There will likely only be enmity.

4. What are you striving to change that you should not be trying to alter?

"Lord, help me to stop trying to change aspects of my life that can become counterproductive."

Trying to make improvements may be in the best of intentions,
But these efforts going awry can result in futile dissensions.

5. What are some aspects of your life that you do not know whether they are changeable or not changeable?

"Lord, help me to have the wisdom to know the difference between what I can change and what I cannot change regarding the aspects of my life."
There are times when the decision is not clear whether something can be changed.

Decision making takes a time of prayerful effort for you to explore,
Making a decision that you will not deplore.

6. How can serenity, wisdom, and courage help me to apply the intention of the powerful dynamics of the prayer?

Imagine what you would look, feel, and act like if you were filled with *wisdom*, living the lifestyle of the Serenity Prayer.

Envision what you would look, feel, and act like if you were filled with *courage* resulting from living the Serenity Prayer lifestyle.

Visualize what you would look, feel, and act like if you were filled with *serenity* resulting from living the Serenity Prayer lighthouse lifestyle.

In each state of wisdom, serenity, and courage, how would your body language look?

What would your facial expression look like?

How would you look out of your eyes?

What would the tone of your voice sound like?

What more would you be accomplishing?

How would you envision people responding differently to you?

How would you project your life to be different today, in one week, in one month, in one year, in five years . . . ? Your life would be different indeed.

Cultivate these feelings. Obtain a vision, and it will turn into a mission—a mission statement that is empowering. One can apply vision and mission statements to the vast array of your present and future challenges. The Serenity Prayer can serve as fission to spark the energy to carry out your missions. Your thoughts, feelings, and behaviors in tune will lead you to making sound decisions.

7. What do I need to change behaviorally regarding the full scope of my life?

"Lord, help me to change my behaviors that I should change regarding the full scope of my life."

First, you need to affirm what you are doing well. Owning these strengths can help you feel swell. You can then take the next step with inspiration. Your life can then begin to flow, and you experience your life's progressive journey with a glow.

8. What do I need to change regarding my feelings and attitudes concerning the complete ramifications of my life?

"Lord, help me to change what I should change regarding my feelings and attitudes concerning the complete ramifications of my life."

Think about the times you have used serenity, courage, and wisdom to help you in the course of your life. This prayer can take you where you are and help you to move more serenely toward a more fulfilling, purposeful living.

The questions at the conclusion of each chapter then serve as tools to help one uncover more of the power of this prayer. The prayer can become more dynamic. These questions and illustrative answers can fuel your own creative thinking regarding how it applies specifically to your life. As a result, these questions can become ingrained as a part of the fabric of the prayer itself. You can gain a handle concerning how to utilize this prayer and, in turn, gain a greater handle on life.

> *Gradually applying the prayer's full dimension*
> *Can help you to reach your life's purposeful intention.*

Chapter 2

The Serenity Prayer:
Recovery and Discovery

*The Serenity Prayer wraps its arms around wisdom and courage
and nurtures these virtues to their fullest expression.
Then recovery and discovery are freed
from imprisoned suppression.*

The Serenity Prayer raises these issues regarding recovery. One needs to know what to strive to change to recover, how to change what one should change, what not to attempt to change, and what one cannot change. Growing in understanding and accomplishing these tasks in recovery takes serenity, wisdom, and courage. The reward will be a more peaceful focus resulting in dynamic life-enhancing discoveries.

You will become more open to uncover the best that life has to offer. You will be propelled to a new level of living with the momentum, resulting from recovery's discoveries. This dynamic life of discovery provides an abundant life through the Serenity Prayer lifestyle. Whatever type of recovery you need or will experience can be helped by this problem-solving lifestyle.

You will gain intangibly and tangibly what you have lost. Some gains will be seen more in your behavior. Other gains will be experienced in your attitude about life. You will also be able to accept what you cannot change regarding recovery and let it go. This letting go induces a gradual healing-grief process. Then, gradually, energies can move toward the future with more productivity and creativity.

> *The challenging journey of recovery may contain growing pains.*
> *The resulting discoveries will result in an abundance of priceless*
> *   gains.*

> *Recovery is not recoiling to status quo.*
> *Recovery is gaining a new status from which to grow.*

As a result, engaging the Serenity Prayer with the issue of recovery can become a profitable soul-searching pilgrimage. The questions at the end of the chapter will help you ponder and apply the issues that this chapter raises. In the process, you will be honing skills that will enable you to apply the prayer to all aspects of your life. Your life will become immersed in the refreshing waters of this powerful, life-changing prayer.

There is a sense in which your entire life consists of recovery and discovery. Even with your best efforts, you can land in rough spots. The good news is that you can make significant discoveries in the midst of your recovery. You can gain more than you have lost. *Your life will blossom in the midst of where it is soiled. This blossoming takes place as you sink yourself into newly discovered fertilized soil. Your recovery will be more than a rebound. Your recovery and discoveries will become boundless.*

The following chapter briefs you regarding how you can successfully utilize the Serenity Prayer for recovery and discovery. The chapter includes poems and prose to undergird your thoughts and actions. Some of the compelling languages will strike home and have a lasting impact. Giving this chapter thought can result in a preponderance of life changes that can be wrought. You will allow yourself to be coached to recover to a life beyond reproach.

> *Putting some of this chapter in rhyme can help the ideas to linger*
> *And help the horseshoe of your life to become a ringer.*
> *As a result some of the thoughts will grab your soul,*
> *And the changes in your life will be breathtaking to behold.*

The Serenity Prayer Promotes Discovery and Recovery

Recovery: Accepting Where You Are Promotes Discovery

You can only recover from where you are.
If you stay in denial, you may increase the size and amount of your
*   lifestyle's scar.*

You cannot recover wishing you were in a different place.
Then you would not look at reality in the face.

You must accept what you cannot change, or your life can become a
*   rough burr.*
The lack of wisdom and focus can result in life becoming a blur.

A commonly told joke is a conversation involving a man asking for directions. He asked, "How do you get there from here?" The respondent declared, "You cannot get there from here." Many jokes are funny because the contents of the humor are absurd. You can only get there from here. That is the starting point. You will not begin to recover unless you begin to accept where you are. Otherwise, where you want to go will be unreachable.

Not facing reality and pretending that the same pattern will not result in the same misfortune is unfortunate. You are denying reality and evading responsibility. You are not forecasting the stormy repercussions of your pattern of behavior. You need wisdom to change the pattern to result in recovery, which will result in a more purposeful living. The rewards will be worth the effort. The Serenity Prayer will provide the needed spiritual foundation for this meaningful lifestyle.

When I eat too much ice cream, I get a stomachache. Yet sometimes I will tell myself that it will not happen this time and put more on my plate. My feeling well is at stake as the ice cream ache continues to keep me awake. I wish then that I had not opened up the gate to let the ice cream in, resulting in feelings that I hate. Then I make things worse by adding a rich chocolate cake. Feeling awful is my fate.

One day I will learn that eating too much ice cream will make me squirm. One day I will say no and free myself from feeling like a worm. One day I will hit bottom and stop this bad habit. By not facing reality, I feel that I can pull out of the hat a magical rabbit. The rabbit is never there to be found. The recovery continues to not become sound. If I keep thinking the rabbit will come out, this denial will prevent me from experiencing the prayerful recovery's clout.

Recovery and Discovery: Promoting a New Way of Life

The Serenity Prayer will help you recover and discover a new lifestyle.
> *These discoveries will provide meaning and freedom as you are willing to go the second mile.*
> *When you strive to change what you cannot change, life becomes off center.*
> *To recover you need a mentor.*

> *The mentor can encourage you to let go.*
> *Then the Serenity Prayer lifestyle will liberate you to dynamically grow.*
> *As a result, this lifestyle will grant what another lifestyle cannot bestow.*

> *Striving to change what one cannot change only brings woe.*
> *When the horse of your life is going in that futile direction one should say "whoa."*
> *Letting go can change one's life by getting rid of burdensome baggage.*
> *Being freed of this load gives room to place new coping tools of recovery in your carriage.*

Recovery: Fueled by Hope and Empowerment

> *It is hope and empowerment that can help recovery to be ignited.*
> *Then hope is spawned by the expression of wisdom and courage as they are united.*

> *Hope, wisdom, and courage are bathed in serenity's sparkling waters.*
> *When wisdom combines with courage, you will gladly follow wisdom's marching orders.*

> Without *hope one's recovery process will dive.*
> *Hope is what keeps the recovery process alive.*

Recovery is Strength Based

For one to enhance hope, recovery needs to build on strengths that you have already.
Focusing on these strengths results in a recovery of growth that is steady.

When your strengths come to the fore,
You will be amazed at what is in store.

The Serenity Prayer: Tailor-made for Recovery

When I was a teenager, I was with my parents in a clothing store to buy a suit.
As the salesman was conniving, my parents did not stay mute.
The salesman wanted to sell me a suit that was baggy.
He said that it could be tailored to make it fit even though it was saggy.

My father said no to the salesman's scheme.
He realized that trying to make the suit fit was just being mean.
The suit was not suitable to adapt to my size.
The salesman was trying to provide good customer service in disguise.

The Serenity Prayer is tailor-made for personal recovery.
It is fit for the challenge to find a lifestyle that is full of discovery.

The Serenity Prayer Provides Guidance for Recovery

Recovery and Discovery: Overcoming Denial

Being in denial renders you helpless to reach the first mile.
Denial has no wisdom to problem solve the trial
As it does not utilize the Serenity Prayer lifestyle.

If there is a hole on the sidewalk, with denial you may go into the hole every time.

You may not be able to approach the hole and stop on a dime.
This plight happens when you repeat your faulty direction.
There is then no one that can give you protection.

You need to look around and find another way.
You may take the advice from another that will help you not to
    sway.
If you wisely change the direction of your steps,
You will learn not to repeat the mishaps.

You can learn the consequences of certain decisions.
Then you will decide not to repetitively go down the same road
    of collisions.
Then you will not have to dig yourself out of a needless hole.
Your life can then truly unfold.

Overcoming denial faces the situation at hand.
The challenges can be handled and can help you to stand.
Whatever obstacles you face, you will be able to withstand.
No longer will denial hold you back.
You will be able to deal with the facts.
Then you will begin the Serenity Prayer lifestyle's appropriate acts.

*Accepting what you can and should change will become your recovery's
    friend.*
Then denying reality will come to an end.
Your Serenity Prayer lifestyle's strong character will not bend.
As you recover, the new discoveries of your life will begin.

The Serenity Prayer: Focus Brings Recovery and Discovery

In recovering in golf, I have found that as my focus has intensified,
I have ended up with the best shots of my life. Once I hit a shot in the
woods. I had the challenge of recovery. I needed to discover a way out of
the trouble. I found a possible way out through a small space between two
limbs. Lining up the shot was difficult as I could not trim the limbs. I had
to go between the limbs to escape from the woods. I was seventy-five yards
from the green. The green had two levels, and the pin was on the top tier.
As I looked over the challenge, I wanted to shed a tear.

I intensified my focus to prepare to recover. I hit the shot through the limbs and did not have to hit another. The ball flew to its freedom and landed on the green. Then, amazingly, it rolled into the hole, and I began to scream. I kept my focus through the process. As a result, I recovered and experienced success.

I would have never found that kind of focus if I were seventy-five yards away from the green in the middle of the fairway. Recovery then can heighten one's sense of focus throughout the day. Wisdom gave me a light to my path, and I successfully negotiated the poor shot's aftermath.

Serenity gave me a presence of mind. Wisdom kept me from being blind. Courage gave me the will to follow through with the plan in my mind. I saw the light and was able to overcome the blight.

What can bring more focus than accepting what you cannot change and changing what you can? Without this attitude, you may find yourself in a situation you cannot stand. I could not change where the ball had landed, but with wisdom, I no longer felt stranded. The negative thoughts were abolished. Hope prevailed and action resulted in mission accomplished. Prayerfully, I was at my best, which laid the challenging problem to rest. I was ready to face the next challenge of life's test.

> *When you feel that your life is stranded where it has landed,*
> *The Serenity Prayer can find you a way out, and your life will become*
> *expanded.*

The Serenity Prayer Provides Recovery Skills

Coping Skills: Tools of Recovery

> Coping skills are tools that can sculpture a life into a work of art
> As one is recovering from a difficult life matter that can truly smart.
> To cope is to keep one's feet on level ground
> As difficult challenges continue to hound.
> Without coping skills recoveries, beginning will not be found.
> With the skill to cope, hope in recovery will abound.
>
> Coping skills such as persistence, determination, faith, and resiliency are just a few

That can keep you from feeling a regretful sense of rue.
Without these coping skills, instead of action
You may feel like you are in traction.

The coping skills of recovery come from being strength based. Think about this scene. A forest is blackened by the blaze of a ferocious fire with soot and embers everywhere. In the aftermath of the devastation, there is a small budding red flower. Building upon the budding flower in the midst of devastation is a strength-based recovery. It is this strength that is recovery's foundation. You need to nourish your budding strengths. Then you will be inspired by the Serenity Prayer lifestyle to go to great lengths. The Serenity Prayer in your heart will continually abide. Needed coping skills are in the Serenity Prayer's lifestyle's positive stride.

Recovery's Demise and Rise: High Self-Esteem Overcoming Low Self-Regard

Low self-esteem can result in a low blow.
Low self-esteem is not interested in seeing your life grow.
While low self-esteem may come from influences from others,
It is ultimately inflicted by your voice within that continually
  bothers.

Positive self-talk can help you recover by walking the talk.
Negative self-talk can be like having a person seeking to self-
  stalk.
You will not be comfortable in your own skin.
The negative self-talk can become incessant with no end.

You need to become a friend to yourself to recover.
Also, you need to become closer to yourself than the finest
  brother.
Self-respect needs to be nurtured with care,
Or the recovery process can be hard to bear.

If weak self-esteem continues to punch low blows without a
  penalty,
In the end the discovery will stay dormant unless you find a
  remedy.

Your talents will not be uncovered as they are scared to come out.
These talents may experience censure that has a powerful clout.

Low self-esteem is interested in recovery's demise.
High self-esteem is excited about a life being on the rise.
High self-esteem begins with a victory within.

As you surround yourself with friends that are cheering for you to win,
They will look at negative self-talk with derision.
This will encourage you to make positive self-talk a powerful decision.

Friends will not accept the self-inflicted low blows.
They will affirm your talents, and you will experience respect that glows.
Because they know the pattern of destructive self-talk can only bring you woes,
They are interested in creating an attitude in which your self-esteem grows.

Feeling good about yourself will no longer feel like a crime.
Self-esteem sparks recovery where discovery will naturally climb.
Then positive self-esteem will make your heart gloriously chime.

Recovery and Discovery: The Serenity Prayer Gives Inspirational Energy

Recovery: Alcoholics Anonymous

Alcoholics Anonymous has inspired the recovery movement with its twelve-step process.
Millions of people have discovered a new lifestyle, which has resulted in success.
These sponsors serve as guides and mentors.
They provide wisdom and inspiration to move one out of a life of rancor.

The person with an addiction realizes that with inspirational
motivation they can cope with their affliction.

A light came on, and they realized what their lifestyle has cost
them.
They had hit the bottom of the barrel and could not recover up
to the rim.
They realized that they could not recover without support.
The sponsor continually gives them healthy guidance with trustful
rapport.

AA provides coping skills needed to help people bounce up from
the pit of despair.
A teachable moment comes when a person begins to really care.
A central part of the recovery program is in helping each person
find spirituality.
Then they become able to recover in actuality.
They find that the Serenity Prayer is spiritual with great
practicality.

They say this prayer at every meeting.
It undergirds the twelve-step program with a sound spiritual
greeting.

In the process of recovery, one has found a new promised land.
They now have a lifestyle that gives them a solid ground on which
to stand.
They are no longer imprisoned inside a corked bottle.
They have access to the power of life's spiritual throttle.

Recovery and Discovery: An Inspiration to Others

If your life of recovery was a life of prose,
The words on the paper would smell like a rose.
Reading about your life of recovery will not result in a doze.
A recovering life is inspirational, energizing people to overcome
their woes.
The inspiration of recovery then continually grows.
As the recovery brightens one's life, another life glows.

Without serenity, wisdom, and courage, one may say, "Cock-a-doodle don't."
Then the need for recovery leaves one saying "I want or I won't."
Because of a wonderful inspiration, one will not be remiss.
One will follow through with one's mission's promise.

It helps you to see someone else successfully strive.
Then you will gain inspiration, empowering others to arrive.
You need to learn how to balance acceptance and change inspired by those who care.
Then you can develop the skills of an inspired life that is the heartbeat of the Serenity Prayer.

The following guiding questions are adapted to the chapter on recovery and discovery. These thought-provoking questions serve as coaches to help you ponder the personal applications and implications of the Serenity Prayer. The resulting soul-searching exercise can aid you to experience the Serenity Prayer lifestyle more fully. The Serenity Prayer then will be a great spiritual resource to help you keep the course.

Coaching Questions to Aid in Applying the Serenity Prayer to Your Recoveries and Discoveries

Remember:

You are not starting from scratch. You have long since been hatched.
In your life, your efforts have not gone for naught.
You can be commended for what you have already wrought.

These questions and thoughts are for the purpose of serving as a personal friend and coach. They can give you the opportunity to prayerfully discover solutions for your personal challenges. You may discover an opportunity to build upon what you are already doing well and take another step forward. This exercise can become a profitable soul-searching pilgrimage.

1. **What do you need to accept that you cannot change regarding the circumstances from which you need to recover?**

"Lord, help me to accept what I cannot change concerning my issues with life matters from which I need to recover."

It is very difficult to let go of the unalterable aspects of life. They can bring you to the altar when you falter in reducing your internal strife. For example, you may experience a plight from which you need to recover. Even if you were not responsible for the difficulty of the plight, you still need to accept responsibility for recovering with all of your might.

2. What do you need to change that you can change regarding your personal recovery?

"Lord, help me to change the things that I should change and help me feel empowered in my recovery." You can make a difference that counts—the worthless behaviors you can renounce. For example, all of us are unfinished pieces of work. One important aspect of this part of the prayer is discerning what you need to change about yourself. Feeling empowered instead of feeling victimized is vital. Feeling responsible in your recovery is paramount.

There may be some things that you may be striving to change in the wrong manner.

"Lord, help me to change the things in the right manner concerning my recovery."

> You can actually make matters worse by striving to recover in the wrong manner.
> Does the manner of change have good manners? Does the manner of change exhibit good wisdom?

It can help by thinking of an example of how you have successfully recovered from a difficult situation in the past. Begin from a positive feeling. Utilize skills that you have used in the past to help you feel more empowered in the present.

3. What are aspects of your recovery that you do not know if they are changeable or unchangeable?

"Lord, grant me the wisdom to know the difference between what is changeable and what is unchangeable in my matters of recovery."

> There are times when the decision is not clear,

Whether something can be changed that is so dear.
This takes a time of prayer and a time to explore,
To help make the decision that one will not deplore.

The Serenity Prayer and information gathering can help. Also, networking with people can gradually bring clarity. God grants wisdom in many ways.

4. **What are some things that you may be striving to change in the wrong manner?**

"Lord, help me to change the things that I need to change in the right manner."

Does the end justify the means?

Is the process worthy of the progress?

Does the manner of change have good manners?

It can help by thinking of an example of what you have changed in a positive manner. Begin from a positive feeling.

When one changes things in the wrong way, there is no serenity.
There will likely only be enmity.

5. **What are you striving to change that you should not be trying to alter?**

"Lord, help me to stop trying to change aspects of my life that can become counterproductive."

Trying to make improvements may be in the best of intentions,
But these efforts going awry can result in futile dissensions.

6. **How can serenity, wisdom, and courage help me to access the power of this dynamic prayer regarding my recovery?**

The Serenity Prayer gives you meaning and purpose

And helps you to live life filled with a surplus.

Imagine what you would look, feel, and act like if you were filled with wisdom regarding your particular recovery.

Visualize what you would look, feel, and act like if you were filled with courage regarding your particular recovery.

Envision what you would look, feel, and act like if you were filled with serenity regarding your personal recovery.

In each state, how would your body language appear?

What would your facial expression be like in each state in successfully recovering from you person matters?

How would you look out of your eyes as you wisdom, courage, and serenity in being successful in your recovery?

What would the tone of your voice sound like?

What more would you be accomplishing and discovering?

How would you envision others responding differently to you as you recover?

How would you project your life to be different today, in one week, in one month, in one year, in five years in the growth that you experienced in your personal recovery . . . ? Your life will be different indeed.

Cultivate these feelings. Acquire a vision, and it will turn into a mission that is empowered. Then your attitude toward you mission will not become soured. Your hopes for reaching your goal will not be devoured. Your growth will be a result of your faith that has towered.

7. What do I need to change regarding my behavior in my recovery?

"Lord, help me to change the things I should change regarding my behavior in my recovery."

It is helpful to affirm what you are doing well.
Owning these strengths can help you feel swell.

You can then take the next step with inspiration.
Then the next step of growth will not be out of desperation.

One can begin to go with the flow.
And experience life's progressive journey with a glow.

8. What do I need to change regarding my feelings and attitudes about my recovery?

"Lord, help me to change the things I should change regarding my feelings and attitudes about my personal recovery." One's attitude is one's life's outlook. If it is negative, it can lead to a donnybrook. If it is positive, it can provide one a life's stance to celebrate each day with the attitude of wanting to dance.

Part 2

The Serenity Prayer:
A Coach for Healthy Family Living

Chapter 3

Taming Control/Change Issues in Marriage

Trying to change one's marriage relationship in the wrong manner
Will not grant one a welcome-home banner.

This banner will surely come down torn,
Canceling the homecoming, leaving both spouses forlorn.

The Serenity Prayer raises these issues regarding marriage. You need to know what to strive to change, how to change what you should change, what not to attempt to change, and what you cannot change. Growing in understanding and accomplishing these tasks in cultivating a healthy relationship certainly takes serenity, wisdom, and courage.

Engaging the Serenity Prayer with the essential aspects of a healthy relationship can become a profitable soul-searching pilgrimage. The questions at the end of the chapter helps you apply the issues that this chapter raises. In the process, you will be honing skills to apply the prayer to all aspects of your life. These skills can prevent needless moaning and groaning regarding marital living.

Nothing flies in the face of intimacy more than control issues. When aspects of control become out of control, they can become a menace to a marriage. Misusing power in an effort to change one's mate can mangle a relationship. As a result, both mates can become entangled.

In the game of chess, the match ends when one player corners the other and gains the position of checkmate. The other player then has no move left. In a spousal relationship, if only one mate wins, the whole relationship loses. Consequently, in the crucial game of life, the move resulting in a checkmate may become "wreckmate." One partner is controlled and cornered. There is no move left. The controlling partner's move may have been seen as being deft. But in the crucial game of life, the relationship may now be over. The wreckage is too severe, disenabling each partner's being a lover.

Control can cause a relationship to sail or rail.
Control can cause a relationship to be sound or to drown.

Often, when couples strive to control each other, communication can become highly conflicted power struggles. The relationship may feel like two porcupines with their quills activated. These quills can become mutually tormenting. If one partner has quills and the other partner has feathers, the feathers may be ruffled.

It behooves both partners to transform their quills into feathers. They can humble themselves and pull out a feather, signifying that they want to come comfortably together. They will change what they should change. Each partner will alter themselves, which in turn influences the relationship.

Each partner will be able to put a relational "feather in their cap."

Then couples can discuss differences with less dissension. The outcome will result in the couple's intention. Communication will have many positive results to mention. The twain shall meet. Mutually comfortable contact can result in relational delight. They may have a playful pillow fight with feathers flying with no fright.

Control matters can bring focus or fret.
Issues of control can cause a relationship to soar or sour.

When stress is managed well, it sets the stage for getting the relational train to get on a healthy track. The climate will become conducive for dialogue. Couples can learn to enjoy coupling and intimacy. Harnessing control can benefit one's mate. The outcome of the marriage then may exude a good fate.

In striving to change what should be changed, bonding and intimacy require that a couple take the reins together in charting the course of their relationship. Both partners need to feel that they have an influence. They both need to feel that they have a voice that is heard and heeded. When the partners do not overcontrol, they allow each one's differences to unfold. Each partner accepts each other's uniqueness. They do not see each one's differences as something to fix. The differences can become a part of the healthy marital mix.

Control issues go awry when the integrity of one partner is compromised by the demands of the other. Love involves demonstrating concern regarding their partner's growth and well-being. The following are two conversations that represent positive and negative communication:

Control can become orders or can influence harmonious order.

Spouse 1: Honey, I am quitting work and going to school to become a lawyer.
Spouse 2: We have not even discussed the matter.
Spouse 1: What is there to discuss? The decision is already been made.
Spouse 2: I will be the one carrying the kids to their activities, and I will spend three times as much time taking care of them.
Spouse 1: You will learn what I have been going through.

When communication becomes nonnegotiable demands,
The relationship can be severed by relentless commands.

When control is not harnessed, one partner's growth is jeopardized. The controlled spouse's development is compromised. The controlling spouse may use their mate for their own needs. Their behavior may be filled with self-serving deeds.

Here is an alternative, kinder, and gentler approach:

When a demand is softened to a preference,
The resulting communication results in a remarkable difference.

A sense of openness will likely ensue,
This openness can keep tension from wanting to brew.

Spouse 1: I am seriously thinking about going back to school and become a lawyer.

Spouse 2: I am so proud of your ambition. I think you will be very successful. We do need to discuss how we are going to divide responsibilities with the children and household chores, etc.

Spouse 1: I know that this is going to place more responsibility on you. I will have to cut back some. We can discuss how we will adjust and come up with some agreeable plan.

Spouse 2: You helped put me through school, and you deserve the same.

Spouse 1: Thank you for caring about a very important aspect of my life.

When communication exudes deep, abiding respect,
A mate may be prevented from wanting to hit the deck.

Resolution can occur when each partner feels respected and safe.
Then a win-win can result in the mates wanting to mate.

A better understanding of control issues can be brought to light by comparing three different kinds of relationships. One relationship is like two circles that are side by side. The circles do not intersect. The relationships contain no abiding respect. There is no relational bond. One partner may strive to communicate, and the other spouse will not respond.

They are more like roommates. In their comings and goings, their lives do not mesh. They may engage in conversation as if they were passing on the street. The conversations may infer that they did not even want to meet. Communication is limited to the needs of living in the same house. Bonding needs are not met. These couples who are not getting along may place activities in between the relationship to keep distance. Discussing time to be together may result in resistance. One may spend more time at work, golfing, separate activities, etc. The affairs of one's life can serve as damaging affairs to the marriage.

Some couples are like two ships passing in the night.
Their beating hearts are out of sound and sight.

With unresolved issues looming, closeness is uncomfortable. Consequently, their lives may move further and further apart until there is no genuine bond. Some couples live like this for years. Other couples may terminate the marriage. A number of couples are able to improve communication and move toward bonding.

Next, there is the circle that intersects. This intersection represents a nice bond with each person's individuality honored. The couple feels that their individual, separate lives are growing while their relationship is strengthening.

> *Some couples are like two ships that are passing in the day.*
> *Their hearts are in sight and are sound as they stop together and*
>   *stay.*
> *Then when they part, they take a piece of the treasure of their partner's*
>   *heart.*
> *The bond is still there even though the two ships have parted*
>   *awhile.*
> *They later return to the dock and give each other a welcoming*
>   *smile.*

Mutually enjoyable activities can help enhance a couple's bond. An example of a relaxing, engaging time is hiking. In hiking, communing with the beauty of nature brings down walls and helps one to commune with each other verbally and nonverbally. Walls come down as stressful distractions fade into the background. The beauty of nature's masterful artwork absorbs all attention and plunges one in the present moment where all that came before and all that will come after is nonexistent.

The present is all that matters, and the foundation for nurturing a relationship is built. Intimacy and closeness are the priceless results. Romance can be expressed by words, but the experience goes beyond words. When no word needs to be said, romance is in its deepest state. A deep connection is mutually felt.

Finally, there is the circle within a circle that depicts one partner overpowering the other. These two circles illustrate when control issues are out of control. The communication is a one-way street. The traffic is only going in one direction. If one partner strives to go down the one-way street, believing it is a two-way road, the partners will collide. One person will be dying inside, and the relationship can become a total *wreck.*

A caricature of the overcontrolling relationship may also be graphically depicted by a Balboa snake coiled around its prey.

Many people in a controlling relationship say that they are feeling smothered because they do not feel safe to be themselves. The partner who is controlling often lives with pain inside. They act out their pain, and the spouse may act in their anguish. To promote peace to avoid conflict, one spouse may agreeably placate.

Unbridled control creates an unhappy spouse. The controlled mate then may experience the partner as a louse. The partner is not a louse. It certainly would not be wise to call the partner a louse even though the partner's behavior may be lousy.

Many marriages end up in a crisis if the controlled partner calls the other partner's hand. They are tired of their partner playing with a stacked deck as they are living with a deck of cards that are stacked against them.

Under this intimidation, one mate may want to "hit the deck." There is a danger that the marriage may dissolve, but there is also an opportunity for true intimacy to take place, creating mutual harmony. Control can cause a relationship to flounder or create a tasty flounder. Control can cause the marriage to be a famine or a feast.

The applecart has been turned upside down. The stage has been set. The partners can pick up the apples and start throwing them at each other. An escalating, conflictive communication pattern may ensue. The overreactive statements may not be true. Both partners can feel very blue.

On the other hand, the partners have the opportunity to put the apples back in the cart in a manner that can enliven their marriage. There is then the possibility for the marriage to be a two-way street. The traffic can flow in both directions. Both voices can be heard. The couple, then, can know they are influencing each other.

As a result, the couple feels that their relationship is being mutually fed.
In this balanced giving and receiving manner, one partner will not
be in the red.
When differences occur, both partners can strive for a win-win.
This form of communication can help deeper intimacy to begin.

One person does not talk and only hear the echo of their own voice.
Listening to the unique voice of their partner becomes an intentional
choice.
The couple does not see their partner as an extension of their own
needs.
They are interested in enhancing the relationship with good deeds.

They realize that listening and respecting the distinct voice of the partner is vital. In communication, you must not catch an idea that the partner has thrown and intentionally dropped the ball and then picked up another ball and threw it back. This detrimental behavior becomes a way to divert attention away from the issue that has been brought to the table. The crisis can be dangerous. If the spouse's different voice is not heard, the calamity can be avoided as the partner listens to every word. The relationship may be bruised if the spouse's request for the partner to listen is refused. Dropping the ball can cause communication to stall. Catching the ball can help communication to become a ball.

Ponder this conversation between the partners of this couple:

> *In the first dialogue, one spouse's voice was not heard or heeded.*
> *In the second, both voices were heard, making each one feel needed.*

Spouse 1: I need to talk with you regarding how you can help more around the house.

Spouse 2: Well, I need to talk with you about how you can be more sensitive to how tired I am when I come home from work.

Spouse 1: That is an interesting response. I have a very demanding job as I work as well. I also do all the housework.

Spouse 2: You need to think about doing more yard work too.

> *One partner side stepping the issue*
> *Can create tears in their spouse, resulting in a need for a tissue.*

This kind of conversation may bring a better outcome.

> *These spouses are dealing with the issue that is brought to the table,*
> *And they are in step with a successful solution because they are able.*

Spouse 1: I need to talk with you regarding how you can help more around the house.

Spouse 2: It sounds like having to do all the housework is very difficult.

Spouse 1: Yes, especially since I have recently received a promotion. I come home and just do not have the energy to do it all.

Spouse 2: What can I do to help?

Spouse 1: It would be a great help if you would wash the dishes after I cook.

Spouse 2: That sounds fair. Is there anything else I can do?

Spouse 1: It is very sensitive of you to ask how you can help. It keeps me from beginning to yelp. Taking out the trash is becoming more difficult for me. That would be a great aid if you would gather the trash and place it in the bin and roll it out to the curb. [*saying with tongue in cheek*] Then, I will not have to kick you to the curb.

Spouse 2: Okay. Let's execute the plan and that and see how it goes.

Spouse 1: That sounds like a plan. I hope I do not get executed.

Responding to the distinctive voice of their partner can create a relationship of distinction.

A couple can feel more relaxed and safe and can infuse relational humor. Not lighting the fuse can result in a positive demeanor. Humor is the positive relational skill that gives a couple a natural high. Wit can create a relationship that says, "My, oh my." Comedy can help prevent a tragedy. The relationship then can become a blissful rhapsody. The mate can sign a love letter "Deliriously yours". Then the fun-filled, healthy, crazy relationship will not feel like chronic chores.

Silliness and seriousness can shake hands to form a more serene relationship. In the right manner, humor can be the oil to prevent inertia and sparks from relational friction. The communication will have good diction. Humor can prevail, keeping the relationship from becoming stale.

The balance between the sublime and the ridiculous can keep the seesaw smoothly going up and down to tickle the partner's stomachs. Silliness can bring serenity, resulting in emotional safety. Safety then can instill a sense of security. Security can culminate in trust, resulting in a strong relational bond.

Trusting can prevent a relationship from rusting
By promoting the oil of humor to lessen needless fussing.

Thus, humor can help one transcend a difficult situation and accept what one cannot change. Laughter, then, reduces stress and helps one to rise above problems that are not solvable. Furthermore, humor can help make the solvable problem more amenable to reveal a solution. Then the words in the air will not feel like pollution. Humor then has many amenities that can keep the relationship spinning. The couple's heads and hearts will be delightfully swimming. The humor can help keep the relationship sound. Then the relationship will not drown.

Coping with thorny issues, with appropriate humor, frees couples to experience a bouquet of laughter and joy. Silliness and serenity can prevail over stress and enmity. As a result, a healthy, crazy relationship can help each partner become crazy about each other. A playful relationship can play into the hands of a good-natured marriage. Control issues can be tamed by a sense of lightness that keeps stress from making marriage a mess.

Pursue Distance: Another Way Control Goes Awry

> The pursue-distance pattern can change when one doesn't feel controlled.
> The pattern needs to be changed before the relationship becomes too old.

Then spouses can say:
"Catch me of you can, and you can. You are the man."

Professional surfers say that their lives are at stake as they ride a wave. As they are surfing the gigantic powerful wave, they have to be very skillful. One wrong move can place them in harm's way. Instead of having the thrill of riding the powerful wave, they could be killed as they helplessly experience the brutal churning of the wave's overwhelming might. The wave can take them under, out of sight.

This scene depicts many men's fear of intimacy. They fear losing their own autonomy and becoming helplessly engulfed in the power of the relationship. A dominating mother may have stifled their growth. Additionally, they may have experienced their mother dominating their father.

The couple can learn to mutually ride the wave. As a result, they will have a relationship to save. Their relationship will not waver. The bonding experience will become priceless to savor. Their mutual intimacy and closeness will be full of flavor.

This relational fear left unattended may result in the man distancing as the wife pursues. As a result, a wife may feel she has no influence. Her pursuit may escalate and intensify. Then, the man may escalate his distancing. The twain shall never meet. When the man distances, the woman feels helpless. As her attempts to engage her husband are discounted, she may feel that her needs are not counted.

She may not be able to influence her husband at all. As a result, she may feel that she is talking to a brick wall. In a relationship, if one partner is always the one to pursue, a relationship that has a widening gap will probably ensue. Then the pursuing partner may begin the conversations with harsher start-ups. The partner may strive desperately to achieve contact, to have some influence on the relationship. The other spouse, feeling vulnerable, may withdraw to avoid a fight. Both have reasons for their behavior.

With the continuation of this negative pursue-distance-communication pattern, this dynamic may intensify. Communication may take the form of blame-withdraw pattern. Fuel is added to the fire when the blame is linked to a feeling that the partner is being irresponsible.

One spouse may scold their partner, resulting in their withdrawing, feeling painfully under attack. As a result, the partner may feel rejected as their requests are not heard or heeded. One partner may feel emotionally battered. The other spouse may feel very tattered. The relationship may be marred as both partners feel profoundly scarred.

The pursue-distance dynamic, which may involve a myriad of issues, may intensify as the feelings of being rejected and used become greater. Thus, each partner may take turns going into hibernation to avoid the painful, failed attempts to bond. One partner may turn a cold shoulder to avoid the painful feeling of being controlled. The other spouse may give up in despair, feeling like they are shouldering the bulk of the work in the relationship.

Many couples find themselves in this pursue-distance relational pattern. This pattern is a futile way of avoiding being controlled. This cat-and-mouse chase can create a fit of frenzy. When the cat is away, the mouse will play. When the cat comes back, it darkens the mouse's day. The hide-and-seek pattern can sour attempts at contact. If this pursue-distance pattern continues, intimacy in the relationship may be in jeopardy.

The spousal relationship is in danger as this negative relational pattern undermines one partner's influence. Thus, control issues can become out of control as one partner has no mutually gratifying impact on the other. There is no opportunity to negotiate a win-win solution. Mutual giving and receiving is null and void.

A couple may exit from this cycle of exile by communicating in a softer tone. This nonattacking tone can be more engaging. The conversational tone may be akin to the way the couple communicated when they were engaged. The cat will no longer be catty and drive the mouse batty.

> The cat will go to bat for the mouse.
> And the cat will no longer act like a louse.

When the cat comes back, the mouse will play.
The cat then will make the mouse's day.

Then they will know that their relationship matters.

There will be cohesion instead of a deep emotional lesion.

Triggers: Learning to Become Trigger-happy

Triggers are vulnerable spots that stem from the past. They are hurt places inside that continue to last. When a partner pushes this button after becoming mad, the mate can become very sad. Being set free from the triggers' trance can set a foundation for cultivating a terrific marital romance.

Getting control issues under control involves understanding triggers. Triggers occur when one partner's behavior or words strike a painful chord in the other's emotional system. The broken string hurts when it is plucked. Instead of providing harmonious music, it can promote

DISCORD

For example, a woman or a man may speak harshly, and the partner may become triggered. Residual underlying feelings lingering from past verbal abuse or painful experiences as a child may erupt. The comfortable communication change will be very abrupt.

Too many pushed triggers can create many rigors. The resulting music is not pleasing to the emotional ears. The painful feelings are reverberations of anguish that one has experienced early in one's life.

These painful feelings are echoing and creating disharmony and static in the present. As a result, a partner may overreact to the situation at hand. On the other hand, one partner may feel like withdrawing and placing their head in the sand.

For example, many people experience abandonment issues. Abandonment feelings occur in many ways for a child. Underlying painful feelings of fear of being cast aside may occur if the adult as a child was abused by someone they trusted. Feelings of being forsaken may also have originated when the adult was emotionally deprived by distancing, disengaged parents.

These underlying feelings of being discarded can play out in a relationship in the form of overcontrol. One partner may strive to overly control their mate for fear of losing them. Intimidation and fear may be used in an attempt to keep the partner under control.

They may beat down their partner emotionally until the partner feels that they have no separate, autonomous self. The controlling partner may treat their spouse like they are extensions of themselves. When one partner asserts their differing opinion, the other partner may strive to gain dominion.

Thus, when one strives to be a unique, separate person, one may feel offensive to the controlling mate. These toxic, hurtful abandonment feelings, in an extreme case, can result in physical or emotional abuse. The broken string of the painful feelings of their past neglect or abuse has been plucked. As a result, severe disharmony in the individual and in the relationship may put the relationship out of luck.

There is an unnerving twang instead of a soothing tune. Subsequently, control issues can hit vulnerable places in the partner in which they are not immune. These vulnerable places of pain being plucked can wreak havoc, resulting in no relational gain. These abandonment sensitivities can become minefields of explosive behaviors that create dark clouds of flooding rain.

When one has been triggered, then one may be quick on the trigger and reactionary bullets may start flying. The relationship may feel like it is in risk of dying. One partner may become too charged up to be in charge of their feelings. At this point, the emotional control issues can become out of control. There may be a gunfight at the OK corral. The person that is emotionally shot may feel like the relationship is wounded, and the infection may drain the affection.

You can utilize a repertoire of ways to calm yourself and become more centered. Deep breathing is a universally effective way of calming one down, as it produces more oxygen in the system. As a result, you can concentrate on your deep breathing. This focus can help stop you from becoming susceptible to seething. Then the OK corral will be OK, and there will be no standoff. The relationship will stand strong as the partners will not do their partner's wrong. The communication will become a harmonious song.

One partner who acts out their pain from the past often marries a partner who acts in their anguish. If this pattern continues, the relationship may be susceptible to perish. The pattern will need to change to save the marriage that they cherish. The person may begin to have difficulty with depression and anxiety. The surfacing feelings from the past may rock one's emotional system. Then the relationship may be threatened by a divisive schism.

A dynamite explosion may occur when people who both act out their pain marry each other. The relationship can become an emotionally and physically volatile bother. This antagonistic couple may feel like relational rubble. They may feel like the marriage is in serious trouble as the emotional needle has popped their bubble.

This relational pattern may be creating potholes for a bumpy, rough ride. The partners may continually, emotionally chide. Counseling may be necessary to help the couple learn to be on each other's side. Counseling may successfully resolve their emotional rigors resulting from the painfully plucked triggers.

No one is to blame their behavior on their past. It is simply important for both partners to be sensitive to their partner's vulnerability, to prevent their relationship from becoming aghast. Then the relationship will not turn into hate before it is too late. The couple will know what is happening when they are triggered. They will have learned to respond in a wise manner that has been wisely figured. They can keep the anguish of one generation from infiltrating their present lives. The couple will experience that their relationship continually thrives. They have learned how to relate to prevent their relationship from taking unrecoverable dives.

For years, couples may have poked at their partner's underlying pain. As a result, a familiar argument resurfaces, which results in no gain. Each partner at different times needs to be the one to stop the fight. Then they will recover from the quarrel right. They may have been stuck in this conflicted pattern for years. Now the change has brought joy instead of sorrow to their tears.

> *Triggers from the past will no longer result in an explosive blast.*
> *Learning how to become trigger-happy can help the relationship to last.*
> *Then living together can become a joyful blast.*

Interdependence: Balancing Control

We all like to be in control. When control issues are out of control, they can ignite a damaging fire in the relationship. When one is overcontrolling, they may be striving to change matters in the wrong way. Also, they may be striving to change matters that they should leave alone. To put out and prevent fires, one must at times let go of always having to be in charge. The understanding of the need to let go control is enhanced by understanding interdependence. Then the ire will not turn into relational fire.

In a healthy relationship, one partner is not always in charge. As a result, each partner's relational influence is very large. Interdependence gives both partners voices. No one person makes all of the choices. There is a difference, then, between being independent, dependent, and interdependent. Moving back and forth from being independent to being dependent in a relationship is called interdependence. Being interdependent is the key to having a balance of control.

When both partners are switching from being in control to giving the partner control, bonding is enhanced. Trust and security in a relationship is needed to relinquish control. One partner may lead in one aspect of a relationship at one time while the other spouse may lead at another time.

Both partners are influencing change agents. Each partner takes leadership in their roles. This partnership creates intimacy between the two souls.

Giving up the reigns in a situation and then taking charge in another circumstance allows both partners to contribute to the relationship. Choosing to rotate control creates a climate for intimacy as both partners are involved in the direction of the relationship. When one moves from being no longer single, the person's life is now related to how the partners intermingle.

To help couples understand the challenges of switching roles, I ask them to do an exercise. One partner is asked to stand while the other partner kneels in front of them. Then, they are to look at each other in the eyes. Next, they let themselves feel what they feel and think what they think. Then, they reverse roles.

Next, they discuss how they feel differently in each role. Couples may have positive and negative feelings in each position. When a mate is locked into a position of always having to be the strong one or being the dependent one, bonding is diminished. The strong one never, or seldom, shows vulnerability or allows the partner to give to him/her. The giving and receiving aspect of the relationship is not intact. One person is always kneeling while the other person is constantly standing.

In interdependence, the partner may give up control of the finances because their partner is much better in handling money. This does not mean that there is no communication regarding financial issues. It means that one partner provides more leadership and time concerning finances.

The couple's bond is strengthened because of the giving and receiving. Then both partners experience receiving the benefits of the other. *It works because it is not against the mate's will. The change will not result in the relationship becoming ill. As it is a mutual decision, the partner's feelings will not be one of derision.* The integrity of the relationship will be intact. The spouse is being tactful regarding how power in the relationship is handled. Then both partners do not feel like they are sitting on a tack.

Sometimes a "rescuer" type personality will marry a "dependent" type. The rescuer may have taken on a giving role early in life to make up for a deficient parent. The rescuer becomes the strong one and is constantly standing. The overachiever and eager beaver's life may become overly demanding. This zealous lifestyle may result in one loathing being so commanding. The pattern may continue if the dependent type is not withstanding.

Stopping always the strong one may be difficult to accomplish. If they don't, they may hear their partners beginning to admonish. In their overzealous efforts to be strong, they may also feel persecuted and in the wrong. Their own needs are not being met. As a result, they may flip into persecuting the partner. Also, when the persecuted partner tries to become strong or assume more responsibility, the rescuer may find fault in what they do in an effort to regain control. Then the cycle continues, and interdependence is sabotaged.

When one person feels they always have to be the one that is strong, the relationship will end up being unhealthily wrong. When a partner becomes tired of always being the strong one, a crisis in the relationship may result. They may feel that not being appreciated is an insult. In the danger of this crisis, there is also opportunity. The relationship has the prospect of becoming more balanced.

A healthy river needs both a feeding stream and an outlet. It needs to both receive and give water. If a relationship only receives, it will become like the Dead Sea and become too salty, unable to sustain life. For relationships to be healthy and enlivened, both must be giving and receiving. Being interdependent, both partners will receive and give. The spouses will feed the relationship, and it will live.

This change requires a discussion about the relational pattern. It may be uncomfortable to begin to change. This discomfort can be reframed as growing pains. The benefits will be priceless. The relational bond will be stronger. Feathers will be sticking out instead of painful quills. Communication will be more comfortable. Interdependence can keep the relationship of giving and receiving in balance. The couple will realize that getting control issues under control matters. Communication will be rid of damaging vices. The relationship will avoid many crises.

Manipulation: Conniving Control

Manipulation can mangle a relationship. Manipulation is a form of striving to be in control. When the partner says no and one wants them to say yes, manipulation can become a formidable weapon. Manipulation strives to change relational matters in the wrong manner. This exploitation pokes at the vulnerabilities of the partner until the partner succumbs to the wishes of the manipulator. The partner may treat their needs as if they do not matter.

> *Manipulation has many stipulations placed on one's mate.*
> *Relational indigestion can occur with the load on the manipulated partner's plate.*

As a result, these stipulations may carry with them the marriage's
fate.

Exploitation creates mistrust and makes the partner cautious.
If the behavior continues, the relationship may become nauseous.

The manipulator is not looking out for the well-being of their partner. The conniving behaviors are devious ploys to push one's partner's vulnerable buttons for personal gain. These deceitful plans are implemented until a mutually fulfilling relationship may not remain. In some underhanded manner, the wily person may lambaste their prey until the bullied one becomes as silent as a lamb.

For example, manipulation occurs when a partner strives to put the partner on a guilt trip. Pushing the right button opens the door, and the partner says yes when they really want to say no. Pressuring the partner by the prick of guilt then becomes a sneaky control technique to get one's way.

One dynamic that makes a partner susceptible to manipulation is the need to please. The need to please may result in the partner being successfully manipulated with ease. One partner allows the other partner to take what they do not really need to give. This can become a pattern the relationship continues to relive. Sacrificial giving is honorable. If but if sacrificial giving is a repetitive knee-jerk reaction with no thought, it can become abominable. This demeaning behavior's emotional and relational damage can become astronomical.

Yes and *no* need to be balanced in dealing with people's demands and requests. Some people virtually say yes to any request or manipulative ploy. The partner has difficulty saying no, and the yes response to any demand is pervasive. The person then may become a doormat for the partner to trample upon. They do not have change matters under control. They give up appropriate power and are not adequately empowered. Therefore, when one partner always says yes, the couple's relationship can end up becoming unhealthily imbalanced.

Another type of person is able to express an appropriate no at times. On the other hand, at other times, their spouse may put their vulnerable button, and they say yes when they wanted to say no. If the partner continues to goad, their mate may feel like saying, "Hit the road."

Manipulation, then, can indeed mangle the relationship. In striving to solve the problem, the relationship can become even more entangled. Both partners have the responsibility to change this pattern. They need to have the courage to change what they can. Respect is the key to keeping control under control. One must respect one's own needs and their partner's needs. Bonding can occur when partners are mutually fulfilling the unique needs of each other. Learning to heed the partner's need will not happen with self-focused greed.

The third way of handling boundaries occurs when the partners can let their *yes* be yes and their *no* be no, resulting in a healthy, balanced relationship. This partner's loyalty to their own needs will abide. They can let their yes be yes and their no be no, resulting in a healthy partner and a healthy relationship. Ideally, it is good to have two partners with doorknobs on the inside. Then the control issues are under control. Each partner has the freedom to say yes and no and will not allow the other to manipulate them into usurping their own autonomy.

Learning how to be assertive and not aggressive gives respect to the wishes of the partner while one strives to fulfill one's own needs. Learning one's rights and respecting the rights of their partner sets the stage for true intimacy. Thus, assertive communication has no room for manipulation.

This partner's loyalty to his/her needs will abide. Both partners will have no need to hide. They can let their *yes* be yes and their *no* be no, resulting in a healthy partner and a healthy relationship. Ideally, it is good to have two partners with doorknobs on the inside. Then the control issues are under control. Each partner has the freedom to say yes and no and will not allow the other to manipulate them into usurping their own autonomy.

Learning how to be assertive and not aggressive gives respect to the wishes of the partner as one strives to fulfill one's own needs. Learning one's rights and respecting the rights of their partner sets the stage for true intimacy. Thus, assertive communication has no room for manipulation.

Assertiveness will knock on the door and accept a *yes* or a *no*. There will be no intruding into the life of the partner without permission. They are expressing their preferences and do not raise the request to the level of a daunting demand. When each partner can accept a *yes* or a *no*, the warmth of the relationship climate helps the couple to grow.

Aggressive behavior runs roughshod over the rights of the partner. Then their constitutional rights to "life, liberty, and the pursuit of happiness" have been violated. Democracy cannot be enjoyed in the home. Tyrannical behavior raises its ugly head. Only one vote counts. The voices of both are not heard in the process of decision making. Equal rights in the constitution, for which our forefathers gave their lives, does not move from the country into the walls of their home.

In a democracy, every citizen has a vote and a voice. Each citizen can decide what their preferential choice is. In a tyrannical marriage, dictatorship allows one person to rule. There is no wisdom in dominating. This behavior becomes foolish. This cruel control may use devious actions to fool their mate. They need to change this harmful behavior for the relationship's sake.

The following is an example of an unhealthy and a healthy way of relating:

Spouse 1: We are going to move to California because I want to be near my family.

Spouse 2: Can't we discuss this matter? The move would set me back greatly in my career. I have worked hard to advance and get a job that is very fulfilling.

Spouse 1: There will be no discussion regarding this matter. You put your career above my needs. That is despicable.

Spouse 2: I just want to discuss the decision. Can we wait until I see what kind of job I can find there?

Spouse 1: No, I can find a job anywhere in the medical field. I can support the family. You do not even need to work. I am going to set up the arrangements for the moving van to come next week. You get to packing or our relationship will be totally lacking. If you do not come along, we can call it quits. I will not tolerate your fits.

In this interchange, a suggestion is to be accepted without question. This demand can create relational indigestion. Only one voice counts. The voice of the other spouse has no value of any significant amount. Here is a more productive alternative scenario.

Spouse 1: I am missing my family and friends. I would like to move to California and be near them. What do you think?

Spouse 2: Honey, moving would be very difficult for me. I have worked hard to get a job that I like, and the advancement in my career has been a long time coming. I am also concerned that living so close to your family could have a negative impact on our relationship.

Spouse 1: There are two concerns that you have about the move. You are concerned about how it would affect your career. You are

<blockquote>

also concerned about how living close to my family would affect our relationship.

Spouse 2: Yes, it would be very difficult for me to get a job in my field at the same level that I am in your hometown. Also, when we lived with your family before, you spent so much time with them that we had little time for ourselves. They came over often and without even calling. Also, you went to visit them almost every weekend.

Spouse 1: What ideas do you have? Do you think that we can have a compromise?

Spouse 2: Yes, if we moved to the big city eighty miles from your family, I think I could find a good job there. Also, having some distance could help us to set better boundaries between our relationship and your family.

Spouse 1: I see what you mean. I think we should put more thought in this decision.

Spouse 2: We can spend time looking at this and other options over the next months and see if we can come to some mutual agreement.

Spouse 1: I like that idea.

</blockquote>

This couple avoided caustic communication creating disillusion. By listening to each other, they began to move toward resolution. There was wisdom in the discussion. Serenity, wisdom, and calmness prevailed. They are exploring what can be changed without having a negative impact. Both voices were heard, and there was openness to dialogue. Respect for both partners' feelings was demonstrated. The couple is on their way to finding a solution that will satisfy both partners.

It is evident then that there needs to be a Declaration of Interdependence in the family, which allows freedom to ring over our land and into the hearts and lives of our families. The Liberty Bell then has meaning for families. When couples ring the Liberty Bell, their relationship will begin to jell.

Wisdom

A marriage is healthy and wise when solutions are skillfully and mutually devised. Wise problem solving is at the fore. There is little, reactive, escalating arguing anymore.

Courage

A marriage is courageous as they face hardships and do not abandon ship. They face the calamity together, and the boat does not overly tip. Learning a new communication skill such as assertiveness can take courage, which demonstrates an expression of one's worthiness.

Serenity

A marriage is serene when there is emotional security and trust. This serenity provides a climate for bonding that is a must. The couple's relationship is serene when silence is golden. There is rich communion because they are mutually respectful of each other's needs.

The following guiding questions are adapted to the chapter on marriage. These thought-provoking questions are to help you ponder the personal applications of the Serenity Prayer. The resulting soul-searching exercise can aid you in more fully experiencing the Serenity Prayer lifestyle as you apply this prayer to all aspects of your daily life.

These questions embodied in the Serenity Prayer then can begin a personal lifelong quest in becoming more skillful in living the Serenity Prayer lifestyle. Then the Serenity Prayer can become increasingly embedded in your life. The prayer can help smooth out the edges of life and prevent your lifestyle from becoming coarse. The voice of your life will not become hoarse. The Serenity Prayer then is a great spiritual resource to help you keep the course.

Coaching Questions: Personally Applying the Serenity Prayer to Your Marriage

Remember:

> You are not starting from scratch. You have long since been hatched.
> In your life, your efforts have not gone for naught.
> You can be commended for what you have already wrought.

These questions and thoughts are for the purpose of serving as a personal coach/friend. They can give you the opportunity to prayerfully discover solutions in your particular situation. You may discover an opportunity to build upon what you are already doing well and take another step forward. This exercise can become a profitable soul-searching pilgrimage.

1. What do you need to accept that you cannot change regarding your marriage?

"Lord, help me to accept what I cannot change concerning my marriage."

It is very difficult to let go of the unalterable aspects of life. They can bring us to the altar when we falter in reducing our internal strife. For example, in a relationship, there may be some things about yourself or your partner that cannot be changed. These characteristics may be preoccupying you to some degree. It is a challenge to let the unchangeable go. Your preferences may not be accepted. It may be unwise to raise these desires to a demand. Acceptance is the key to unlock the door to one's partner's heart.

"Lord, help me to accept what I cannot change."

If one agrees to disagree, acceptance of the unchangeable is involved. The issue is likely to be resolved. One can learn to choose their battles and not react to every annoyance or disagreement. The relationship is not stuck on the issue. If one partner leaves on a trip, one will still say, "I will miss you."

2. What do you need to change that you can change regarding your part in the marriage relationship?

"Lord, help me to change the things that I should change regarding my involvement in my marriage relationship."

We can make a difference that counts. The worthless behaviors we can renounce. For example, all of us are unfinished pieces of work. One important aspect of this part of the prayer is discerning what you need to change about yourself. You cannot change your mate, but changing yourself can change the relationship communication pattern.

3. There may be some things that you may be striving to change in the wrong manner.

"Lord, help me to change the things in the right manner concerning my relationship in my marriage."

Does the end justify the means?

Is the process worthy of the progress?

Does the manner of change have good manners?

It can help by thinking of an example of what you have changed properly. Begin from a positive feeling. Then, look at aspects of your life that need to be changed. When one changes things in the wrong way, there is no serenity. There will likely only be enmity.

One can share preferences to ask for change. *Would you?* This way of communicating can be much more receptive than a demand such as, "If you do not stop doing . . ." Of course there are some things you cannot tolerate at all. One partner should not say at the end of the chapter can help you to ponder and apply the issues that this chapter raises. In the process, you will be honing skills that will enable you to apply the prayer to all aspects of your life.

4. What are aspects of the relationship that you do not know whether it is changeable or not changeable?

"Lord, grant me the wisdom to know the difference between what is changeable and what is unchangeable in my marriage."

There are times when the decision is not clear, whether something can be changed that is so dear. This takes a time of prayer and a time to explore, to help make the decision that one will not deplore. The Serenity Prayer and information gathering can help. Also, networking with people can gradually bring clarity. God grants wisdom in many ways.

5. How can serenity, wisdom, and courage help you to access the power of this dynamic prayer regarding your marriage?

The Serenity Prayer gives us meaning and purpose
And helps us to live life filled with a surplus.

Imagine what you would look, feel, and act like it you were filled with wisdom regarding your marriage.

Visualize what you would look, feel, and act like if you were filled with courage regarding your spousal relationship.

Envision what you would look, feel, and act like if you were filled with serenity regarding your marriage.

In each state, how would your body language appear?
What would your facial expression be like in each state in communicating in your marriage?

How would you look out of your eyes as you relate to your wife with wisdom, courage, and serenity?

What would the tone of your voice sound like?

What more would you be accomplishing?

How would you envision others responding differently to you?

How would you project your life to be different today, in one week, in one month, in one year, in five years . . . ? Your life would be different indeed.

Cultivate these feelings. Acquire a vision, and it will turn into a mission—a mission statement that is empowered. You can apply a vision and a mission to the vast array of your present and future challenges. The Serenity Prayer can serve as a fission to spark the energy to carry out the mission of helping your marriage to grow.

6. What do you need to change regarding your behavior in your marital life?

"Lord, help me to change the things I should change regarding my behavior in my marriage relationship."

It is helpful to affirm what you are doing well.
Owning these strengths can help you feel swell.

You can then take the next step with inspiration.
Then the next step of growth will not be out of desperation.

One can begin to go with the flow
And experience life's progressive journey with a glow.

7. **What do you need to change regarding your feelings and attitudes
    in your marriage?**

"Lord, help me to change the things I should change regarding my
feelings and attitudes about my marriage."

Chapter 4

Teenagers: Harnessing their Energies with Wisdom and Courage

Teenage years can bring their parents to tears.
Parents deserve support to alleviate their fears.

Parents need the coaching of the Serenity Prayer
Then it may help them to see parenting as being fair.

Parenting a teenager becomes serene
When parents see a budding adult on the scene.

The Serenity Prayer raises these issues regarding parenting teenagers. You need to know what to strive to change, how to change what you should change, what not to attempt to change, and what you cannot change. Growing in understanding and accomplishing these tasks in parenting teenagers takes serenity, wisdom, and courage.

Engaging the Serenity Prayer with the issue of parenting teenagers can become a profitable soul-searching pilgrimage. The questions at the end of the chapter help one to ponder and personally apply the issues that this chapter raises. In the process, you will be honing skills that will enable you to apply the prayer to all aspects of your life.

It is particularly challenging to keep one's serenity during one's children's teenage years. The adolescent years entail a complex mixture of behaviors. Dealing with control issues comes to the fore. These issues of authority create louder decibel levels of rebellion as the teenagers are struggling for their independence. The following scenario is an example of a teenager who was relishing being in charge.

The counselor asked, "How is it going with your teenage kid?"

The parents replied, "It seems that our kid won't stop wagging the tail of the dog. Why do you think he get so much joy out of that strange behavior?"

The counselor said, "The answer is simple. Your teenager's behavior is demonstrating that he treats you as his parents like he is treating his dog. Instead of the dog (which represents you as his parents) wagging his tail (which is the teenager), the teenager is wagging the dog (which is you as his parents). Your teenager is obviously in charge of you as his parents. That will be $100 please."

Many parents of teenage kids may feel that the tail is wagging the dog. Consequently, this can be a very tough, scary, and confusing time. Teenagers love to push their parents to see how far they can go. It is up to the parents to know when to say whoa. How much freedom to give to teenagers is not always clear. The parents are in charge of their child that they hold so dear. They resist giving unending rope for teenagers to crash and burn. They want to give enough rope to help teenagers learn. The teenager can experience this stage of life in a variety of ways.

I once saw an old man riding his motorcycle. On the back bumper sticker displayed this message, "I am a recycled teenager." Evidently, there was something about his teenage years that he wanted to recapture. He wanted to go back to the good old days. We might speculate that he longed to recapture a carefree time of long ago.

On the one hand, teenage years can be seen as simpler times. It can be a time of unencumbered idealism. Life can seem to be neat and tidy. Excitement has not yet been mellowed by realism. Teenagers may see the solutions of the world as not being so complex. The world may be seen through rose-colored glasses.

In the latter '60s and early '70s, the hippy movement is an extreme example. They were going to find their sense of control by separating from the world and saying that love will conquer the world. It was unencumbered idealism, and then the movement crashed and burned with drugs and a lifestyle that did not balance realism, freedom, and responsibility.

When I was in high school, I overheard the football coach telling one of his players that he should enjoy his time in high school because that was the best time of life. Other people have said that they would not go back to their teenage years for any amount of money. It seems then that for some, teenage years are the highlight of their lives, and for others it is their darkest period.

If we did a poll, most people would probably fall in between. Emotions of typical teenagers can go from one spectrum to the other. Feelings can rise as high as a kite and then plunge to the pit of despair. While in one moment they may see the world through rose-colored glasses, in the next instance, they may see the world through darkened spectacles. They can then make a spectacle of themselves.

These strongly tinted glasses may cast a shadow over their life's terrain. The roller-coaster ride of these youthful days creates a dilemma for our society. Their unpredictable emotions and behaviors present tough challenges for the teenagers and their families.

At the crest of my teenage roller-coaster ride, I experienced carefree times—times of riding my bicycle down the hill near my house. I enjoyed serene times of fishing at the river.

One mountaintop experience occurred when I had the thrill of sinking a thirty-five-foot putt in golf, which led our high school them to victory over a much larger school in a golf match. I scored a 74, my lowest score in competition on a very difficult course. When I played the trumpet in my high school band, chills went down my spine.

Also, my emotions were exuberant when I experienced unencumbered idealism. In my naiveté, I felt that the Christian faith could quickly solve the social ills of the world. I would become elated that I could be a part of stemming the tide of social concerns. The excitement of high ideals was pure and not yet mellowed by realism.

I also experienced the valleys of the future shock of contemplating what I would do with my life. My identity was not intact. In earlier times when teenagers helped out on the farm, there were no in-between years that create identity confusion, which accentuate the age-old question, who am I? Today's teenage challenges are made all the more difficult as they face the future shock of a more complex world, while at the same time they struggle with such issues as physical changes, peer pressure, authority, autonomy, and competency.

Not having a sense of identity can feel like playing the game pin the tail on the donkey blindfolded or playing blindman's bluff. A teenager may try to bluff his/her way through life as a part of the learning process.

The teenager may feel little control over his or her life and wonder how they are going to find their niche in the world. The parents can feel that their family is out of control during this likely turbulent time. The challenge of parenting teenagers may take away more energy than the relationship gives. This pop quiz may leave parents bewildered, frustrated, and emotionally drained. They wonder if they will ever pass the exam. They may speculate with fear what may become of their teenagers when they leave home.

As a result, the parenting task can become the worst of times instead of the best of times when power struggles escalate. It is frightening for parents to let go and allow their teenager to have some freedom to learn from their mistakes. This is a risky period. The parents may try to feel like they should have more control and feel guilty when their teenager strays from the narrow path. It is important for parents to be in charge without being too charged up. Getting entangled in a power struggle is certainly one way to become too intense. The circuit of the family system can become overloaded without a circuit breaker to put on the breaks.

One type of parent that may be especially susceptible to becoming too charged up may not give the teenager adequate room to breathe. These parents do not distinguish between being responsible to their teenagers and being responsible for them. Feeling like they are responsible for their teenagers' lives may create undue intensity. This intensity, which may ignite their child's behavior, reflects directly upon the parents' adequacy. They may then act as if their teenagers are extensions of themselves, resulting in an overcontrolling parenting.

When control issues become out of control, power struggles can ensue. The parenting task can become the worst of times instead of the best of times when power struggles escalate. Communication can spiral out of control as emotions become too extreme to harness. The harness has fallen off, and the horsepower is going out into the wild blue yonder. When parents do not give teenagers room to breathe, teenagers may begin to increasingly seethe.

It is hard to allow the teenagers to have increasing freedom. Letting go of some unwarranted control as parents can create growing pains in the parenting challenge. This challenge is a significant part of the parents' working themselves out of job.

I remember taking my daughter when she was sixteen years old to the beach for a father-daughter time. I saw a man with three children. The children looked to be around two, three, and four years old. He had them on a leash. This was a cute scene. The picture is etched in my memory. He was keeping close watch on his precious children in the midst of the beach crowd. They were walking in front of him, smiling with delight. The control gave them a sense of security.

Later that day, I took Carol to Hartsville, South Carolina, to show her Byerly Hospital where she was born. I asked her to stand in front of the hospital while I took her picture. While she was posing, a teenager drove by and honked his horn. Then, again he turned around and honked. As he passed by a third time, he gave his horn a final blast. I then walked up to my daughter and told her in jest, "I am going to put you on a leash!"

We do become frightened concerning our teenagers, but we must not become so intrusive that we inhibit their growth. They need to learn from their mistakes. Becoming an adult can become overwhelming if they have not been experiencing increasing responsibility regarding their behavior. Age-appropriate consequences have not given them food for thought. This malnourishment has resulted in behavior that has not been fully digested or thought through.

When an infant is one month old, the parents are responsible for virtually every aspect of the baby's life. As the child grows older, the child begins to have more of a percentage of the responsibility of their lives. When a child is twenty, the parents have very little responsibility. It is this letting go and working oneself out of a job that is the parenting challenge.

During teenage years, it is difficult to give teenagers age-appropriate freedom. However, overcontrolling may escalate the teenager's rebellious power struggle. Needless power struggles can ensue if the parent tries too hard. They will not know when the ball is in their teenager's court. For example, if a parent continually yells at a child for not making good grades and incessantly screams at the child for not studying, the parent is crossing the line.

The parent is then feeling responsible for the grades of the child. The parent will not put the ball in the teenager's court. The teenager may feel powerful: "See how angry I can make my parents." The teenager may actually focus more on the parent's furor rather than reflecting on their own irresponsible behavior.

Backing off may allow the teenager to begin to experience more natural consequences of their behavior. Instead of focusing on the intense behavior of the parent and how they can jerk their parents' strings, they will have to think about their own behavior and the resulting consequences. Backing off and putting the ball in the teenager's court gives the adolescent an opportunity to become more responsible.

Parents who feel that they are responsible for their teenager's behavior may become overzealous, feeling that they have to be their savior. Then the teenager does not feel as responsible for their miscues. They may feel powerful as their parents blow a fuse. They may say, "Look how much I can make my parents explode. I do not have to worry because they are taking the load."

If the parents give age-appropriate guidance, the teenagers will begin to have to use their own sense. Their court will now receive the ball, and they will have to face the consequences of their fall. Then they can benefit from the learning curve that may prevent a future dangerous swerve. Teenagers have to learn to forge their own path. Giving guidance then without being too intense can allow teenagers to think for themselves. Then they can find their own unique place in this world.

Listening more than lecturing can also help reduce stress and lessen power struggles. Often, if parents simply listen to their teenagers, their children are more likely to become empowered to solve their own problems.

A parent might ask their teenager how they would rear a sixteen-year-old child and sit back and simply listen and not jump in and judge. Power struggles are reactive, knee-jerk reactions that bypass thought. Giving teenagers some breathing room can help them to think for themselves. By lending them your attentive, nonjudgmental ears, they can problem solve as listening to them has allayed their fears.

The process of backing off and listening can instill more healthy independence. Teenagers can begin to become less reactionary and think more clearly. Instead of having power struggles, they may become more empowered. They will then be on the path of becoming responsible adults. The parents will be working themselves out of a job.

Parenting: Keeping the Fish in the Water

Parents need to provide age-appropriate structure
To keep the family from experiencing a damaging rupture.

On the other hand, some parents may have the opposite parenting style. They may not provide the teenager the structure that they need. The teenager's life may become out of control, and the resulting behavior will be very risky. Teenagers need solid parents to help give them age-appropriate structure and discipline.

While some parents are overprotective and overcontrolling, some parents are underprotective and give too little structure. These parents have difficulty setting limits. *This lack of will to go against the wishes of the teenager is illustrated by this story.*

One time there was a man who went to a pet shop to find a pet for his home. He noticed a cute goldfish swimming in a small bowl. As his eyes met with the fish, there was an immediate connection. He bought the goldfish and took him home.

The goldfish enjoyed the new environment. To his delight, the man discovered that the goldfish could talk. The goldfish initially enjoyed the small bowl, but soon began complaining and wanted more freedom. The man, in an effort to honor the fish's wishes, immediately rushed out and bought a more spacious aquarium. It was large like what a restaurant uses to enhance the ambience of fine dining. The fish was delighted with his newfound freedom.

Then, after a few weeks, he began to complain that he was growing tired of this place. He stated that the glass walls were closing in on him, and he needed more space. He said that he was becoming spaced-out. The owner was baffled at the fish's anguishing cry. His heart went out to him.

An extra bathtub, he felt, might pacify the increasing dissatisfaction of the fish. He filled the tub with water, and the fish was delighted with his larger new home. His pet did not feel as restricted. The restrictions were tempered by the freedom that he felt in swimming in a larger area.

To the dismay of the owner, after a few weeks, the newfound freedom became stale, and the fish stated that the walls were caving in on him. He began to chronically complain about his jail-like living quarters. The pet fish said to the owner that he felt like a prisoner held in captivity.

Again, the owner succumbed to the fish's tearful plea. He felt sorry for the fish's plight and wanted to do everything he could to help the fish to feel happy. Since it was in the summertime, he decided to put the goldfish in his huge backyard pool. Certainly, he thought that this would provide a lifelong, fulfilling experience. When the fish dove into the pool, he was as happy as a lark. He enjoyed his huge pool and his increased freedom.

His happiness was characteristically short-lived as he began to pout with arrogance, exclaiming, "I am going to die if I do not receive more space and freedom!" He exclaimed that he felt he was in solitary confinement and needed more space to free him from that unbearable experience.

Tears began to stream down the owner's face. The plight of his pet fish felt like a plague on his heart. If unlimited freedom was what he wanted, that was what his precious pet was going to receive. The owner impulsively picked up the fish and placed him in his backyard. The fish, with unlimited freedom, quickly breathed its last breath.

The owner did not have the will to go against the wishes of the fish. The fish had no one to set limits to his freedom's unquenchable wish. The fish was determined to get his own way, and his determination caused his owner to succumb, resulting in great dismay.

Parents need to give age-appropriate limits and structure until they gain inner controls. Teenagers need to stay in the water if they are going to be able to swim toward the goal of responsible adulthood.

Catching Teenagers' Good Behavior

As parents, we have the tendency to catch our children doing things that may be detrimental. It is important catching them doing constructive things as well to enhance their sense of competency. This affirmation can also help them discover their special talents. I remember writing a poem in high school that was selected to be placed in a magazine as a memorial for Robert Frost. That positive affirmation lingers with me today and has contributed to developing my writing skills.

Think of the many ways you can affirm your teenager. "You have a knack for that. That comes easy and natural for you."

Helping to water the seeds of their gifts can enable them to look into the future with hope as they develop their sense of competency in the present. They will become empowered to change what they can to enhance their possibilities. Also, they will have the serenity to accept what they cannot change, which is their limitations. Teenagers need to know that they can do something well. This gives them a sense of confidence that can feel so swell. These positive feelings can enhance their self-esteem. Then they will grow into adulthood purposeful and serene.

Having a sense of values, competency, and identity can give a teenager a sense of direction. It is important for teenagers to gradually gain a sense of direction for their lives. The teenager may not know every little detail. They will begin to cultivate a general direction that will enable them to begin to think beyond the present moment. As a result they can dream and set realistic goals.

Teenagers then can declare their "Declaration of Independence" in a healthy sense, as parents have successfully worked themselves out of a job. The teenagers can leave the nest and can now fly on their own and do their best. They are now emotionally, physically, and behaviorally grown. The parents no longer have a need to moan.

Teenagers: When Irresponsibility is Not What It Seems

There are some complicating factors that require different solutions. Sometimes when a teenager's behavior seems to be irresponsible, it may be complicated by depression or attention deficit disorder (ADD). These maladies may create difficulty for the teenager to focus.

The downturn in their grades may not be a lack of discipline. The decrease in motivation and the sense of apathy that the teenager is demonstrating may be symptoms of depression. If the teenager is losing interest in activities that once brought him great joy, he/she may be depressed. Also, the teenager may be withdrawing more to his room.

Another possible symptom of depression is waking up early. The resulting lack of sleep can also hinder concentration. This sleep deprivation can also contribute to a downward spiraling of function and increasing depression. Furthermore, with teenagers, depression may surface as an aggravation. They may become disruptive in school or explosive at home. The level of anger is more than is usual. The mood swings are more pronounced. Consequently, if other symptoms of depression are coinciding with behavior that seems irresponsible, the teenager may need to be seen by a therapist. A therapist can assess whether the teenager is actually clinically depressed and can provide guidance in treatment.

Also, with the rise of suicides among teenagers, it is important to take the teenager for immediate emergency evaluation to assess the level of danger for self-harm if suicide thoughts are emerging. Suicide thoughts have to be taken seriously. If the teenager is bluffing for manipulative reasons, responding quickly to obtain further evaluation can often take the wind out of the sails of this behavior.

Another challenge that can make irresponsible behavior different than it appears is attention deficit disorder or attention deficit hyperactivity disorder (ADHD). While this diagnosis is difficult to ascertain and should not be given too quickly, it needs to be ruled out if certain traits are present. In ADD, the mind is racing. In ADHD, the mind and body are racing.

A person with ADHD may have impulsive behavior at some level. If a child truly has ADHD, the normal discipline measures will only serve to lower the self-esteem of the child. A person with ADD typically receives much negative feedback from family, friends, and teachers, which can dramatically affect their view of themselves.

Teenagers' future shock of moving into the adult world can be intensified if these challenges go undiagnosed. The abilities that the teenager has may be hidden by an avalanche of criticism of what appears to be irresponsibility. If a parent suspects that a teenager may have depression or ADHD, professional help could be needed.

Wisdom

Parenting teens is wise when one disciplines enough but not incessantly. Teenagers need enough structure and room to learn responsibility.

Courage

Parenting teens is courageous when one gives them age-appropriate freedom. They need to learn from both their good and bad deeds.

Serenity

Parenting a teenager is serene when the parents see a budding, responsible adult on the scene.

The following guiding questions are adapted to the teenagers. These thought-provoking questions are to help you ponder the personal applications and implication of the Serenity Prayer. The resulting soul-searching exercise can aid you to more fully experience the Serenity Prayer lifestyle as you apply this prayer to all aspects of your daily life.

These questions embodied in the Serenity Prayer can then begin a personal lifelong quest for you to become more skillful in living the Serenity Prayer lifestyle. Then the Serenity Prayer can become increasingly embedded in your life. The prayer can help smooth out the edges of life and prevent your lifestyle from becoming coarse. The voice of your life will not become hoarse. The Serenity Prayer then is a great spiritual resource to help you keep the course.

Coaching Questions: Personally Applying the Serenity Prayer Regarding Parenting Teenagers.

Remember:

You are not starting from scratch. You have long since been hatched. Your efforts have not gone for naught. You can be commended for what you have already wrought.

These questions and thoughts are for the purpose of serving as a personal friend. They can give you the opportunity to prayerfully brainstorm, to surface the challenges and solutions, and to take another step forward. Engaging and utilizing the Serenity Prayer as a coach with the issue of parenting teenagers can become a profitable soul-searching pilgrimage.

1. **What do you need to accept that you cannot change regarding your teenage children?**

"Lord, grant me the serenity to accept what I cannot change regarding my teenage children."

It is very difficult to let go of the unalterable aspects of life. They can bring us to the altar when we falter in reducing our internal strife. One may wish that their son or daughter would study more, be better at a sport, be more ambitious, or help more around the house. One can provide some consequences to behavior, but a parent cannot force the change to happen.

2. What do you need to change that you can change regarding your teenage children?

"Lord, grant me the wisdom to know what I need to change regarding parental issues with my teenage children."

We can make a difference that counts and the worthless behaviors we will renounce. One may need to change an aspect of their parenting style. For example, one may need to choose their battles with teenagers.

3. What are some things you can change that you may be striving to change in the wrong manner with your teenage child?

"Lord, help me to know where I am going wrong regarding striving to change parental issues with my teenage child."

Does the end justify the means?

Is the process worthy of the progress?

Does the manner of change have good manners?

It can help by thinking of an example of what you have changed in a good manner? Begin from a positive feeling.

When one strives to make changes in the wrong way, there is no serenity. There will likely only be enmity. One may try to be overcontrolling with a teenager, trying to make them become what one wants them to be, instead of allowing a teenager to find their own unique path.

4. What are you striving to change that you should not be trying to change regarding your teenage child?

"Lord, grant me the wisdom to know what I am striving to change that I should not be trying to change regarding my teenage child."

To be nosy can become very noisy. Trying to make improvements may be in the best of intentions, but these efforts can result in futile dissensions. One may not be giving teenagers the privacy that they need.

5. What are some things that you do not know whether they are changeable or not changeable regarding your teenage child?

"Lord, grant me the wisdom to know what should be changed and what cannot be changed regarding my teenage child."

There are times when the decision is not clear whether something can be changed that is so dear. This takes a time of prayer to grant one an opportunity to explore to help make the decision that one will not deplore. How is a parent to respond to a behavior in the teenager that is getting him into trouble? For example, at some point, one needs to place the ball in the teenagers' court and allow them to feel the consequences in tough love.

6. How can serenity, wisdom, and courage help enlighten you regarding parenting issues with your teenage child?

"Lord, help me to fully utilize the powerful resources of serenity, wisdom, and courage to help enlighten me regarding the parenting challenges of parenting my teenage child.

> *The Serenity Prayer gives us meaning and purpose*
> *And helps us to live life filled with an overflowing surplus.*

Imagine what you would look, feel, and act like if you were filled with wisdom concerning parenting your teenager.

Visualize what you would look, feel, and act like if you were filled with courage regarding parenting your teenage child.

Envision what you would look, feel, and act like if you were filled with serenity regarding raising your teenage child.

With each trait regarding parenting your teenage child, how would your body language appear?

What would be your facial expression?

How would you look out of your eyes?

What would the tone of your voice sound like?

What more would you be accomplishing?

How would you envision others responding differently to you?

How would you project your life to be different today, in one week, in one month, in one year, in five years . . . ? Your life would be different indeed.

Cultivate these feelings. Develop a vision, and it will turn into a mission—a mission statement that is empowered. One can make a general mission statement. One can apply a vision and a mission to the vast array of present and future challenges. The Serenity Prayer can serve as fission to spark the energy to carry out the plan.

7. What do I need to change behaviorally regarding parenting my teenage child?

"Lord, grant me the wisdom to know what I need to change behaviorally regarding parenting my teenage child."
It is important to affirm what you are doing and have done well. Owning these strengths can help you feel swell. You can take the next step with inspiration. Then, the next step of growth will not be out of desperation. One can begin to row with the flow and experience life's progressive journey with a glow. One may realize when the teenager is just trying to get a conflict started by pushing buttons. One may stop overreacting to the situation.

8. What do I need to change regarding my feelings and attitudes in parenting my teenage child?

"Lord, grant me the wisdom to know what I need to change regarding my feelings and attitudes concerning parenting my teenage child."
One's attitude is one's life's outlook. If it is negative, it can lead to a donnybrook. If it is positive, it can provide one a life's stance to celebrate each day with the attitude of wanting to dance. One may feel that every mistake

that the teenager makes is a reflection on the parent's ability to parent. That is not true. That kind of attitude can create overreaction to situations, battling behaviors that do not need to be battled. Putting the ball in their court can prevent one from feeling embattled. You will not easily become rattled.

Chapter 5

Stepping into Stepfamily Living with Wisdom

Bringing two families together
Can create stormy weather.

The Serenity Prayer raises these issues regarding stepfamily living. You need to know what to strive to change, how to change what you should change, what not to attempt to change, and what you cannot change. Growing in understanding and accomplishing these tasks in stepfamily living certainly takes serenity, wisdom, and courage.

Engaging the Serenity Prayer with the issues of stepfamily living can become a profitable soul-searching pilgrimage. The questions at the end of the chapter can help you to ponder and personally apply the issues that this chapter raises. In the process, you will be honing skills that will enable you to apply the prayer to all aspects of your life.

Stepping off on the right foot in stepfamily living is, for the vast majority, quite challenging. Often the venture can feel like stepping off a cliff, losing control, tumbling down, and ending up with bruises and scrapes that create lingering pain. The adventurous scenarios of stepfamily living can be a cliff-hanger. One may not know what is coming next, celebration or rancor.

At the beginning, embarking upon a new family can seem exciting. The anticipation can appear very inviting. The vision of the newly merged family can look like unwrapping a present with gorgeous, colorful paper wonderfully decorated with a matching bow. Unfortunately when the bow comes off and the package is unwrapped, the gift inside can seem more like unwrapping a surprise gag gift that is not funny. It can feel like opening up Pandora's box, which contains an overwhelming, complex set of challenges. One would prefer that the surprise gift be a jack-in-the-box. Humor could lighten the box, which contains heavy hearts that feel like rocks.

Stepping into stepfamily living then can have a promising beginning. After recovering from a divorce, it can be seen like an oasis in a desert. This new relationship has great hope from the knowledge gained. It is encouraging that family relationships will be more harmonious. It seems like a wonderful second chance for successful family living. In reality, the stepfamily can begin far-out of step. Stepping into stepfamily living often means stepping on toes. Being out of step can create an untold amount of woes.

These difficulties can overwhelm family living. Family members can feel helpless regarding gaining a sense of harmonious direction. It is helpful to understand the inherent challenges of stepfamily living and accept them. Then stepfamily living can successfully manage the monumental matters. As a result, the stepfamily will deserve a monument as a tribute and testimony for excellence in the quality of the family's relationships.

Trying to ride a bicycle for the first time can be an enormous challenge. One can have difficulty feeling a sense of control, especially around curves. There are learning curves in stepfamily living. Curveballs can be thrown when a family strives to negotiate life's curves. Complex dynamics can feel like dynamite explosions.

The learning curve can be managed. First of all, it involves accepting what one cannot change. Many aspects of stepfamily challenges cannot be changed. Each family member may still be reeling from losses. These unchangeable aspects may be hard to come to terms with.

Therefore, these losses intermingle with present issues and results in heightened complexity. No one feels the losses and the sense of being out of control more keenly than the children. These losses need to be understood to prevent the children's feelings from ricocheting and creating a chasm in the couple's relationship.

Both parents have gone through changes that resulted in loss or were beyond the step of their control. The losses are innumerable. They include a loss of identity, friends, finances, and a loss of the familiar. Changes seem endless in the adjustments that they face. Losses that children have experienced may include not seeing one parent on a daily basis. They may have lost a school, playmates, and neighbors that created roots and familiarity in their lives. Thus, the new marriage may feel like a disruption to most of what they have called dear.

Also, the children may have adjusted to the life of the single parent. This situation provided more one-to-one attention from each parent. Then remarriage upsets the applecart. It threatens the closeness that they experienced in single-parent living. In single-parent living, after the children have been adjusting, a move to stepfamily living may result in feeling like their lives are rusting. The stepfamily may feel as if it is busting. At its worst, stepfamily living may feel disgusting.

Children then may try to create a rift between their mother and stepfather. The applecart can become out of control. The apples may spill out and begin rolling in different directions. The family members can seem as if they are going in different directions trying to find the apples. Chaos and confusion can result. The adjustments in stepfamily living may not seem adjustable. As the temperature rises, the family may feel combustible.

The second-marriage relationship may be a better match than the first. But the complexities of dealing with stepfamily matters can wear away the fibers that hold the marriage together. The foundation may be rattled by a quake. The marriage and family life have the challenge to prevent upcoming aftershocks. The relationship that once felt so together can move toward the brink of destruction. The marriage can become very tattered, and the couple can feel emotionally battered. Then they may feel that their marriage has shattered.

It is commonly reported that three out of four second marriages fail. The increase in the divorce rate is related to the complexities of adjusting to bringing two families together. You are not a statistic. Your family can be successful. These statistics make the point that success is challenging and should not be taken for granted.

Experiencing serenity in the midst of stepfamily living may feel impossible. One must not think that serenity has to be perfect. It is a process of adjusting that will have its ups and downs. The dynamics of family living may go up and down on the serenity scale. One may feel like the chaos is becoming overwhelming. Then calm can come after the storm. Then the storm may come again. Stepfamily living at some points can feel like a placid lake. Then there can be a rumble, and the family can begin to quake. As a result, the family members can become frightened and can shake.

It is difficult to be at peace with oneself in the midst of the changes. This is a normal process. It is important for one to have a place of refuge within oneself where serenity can be experienced. A peaceful detachment and disengagement can be helpful. Then, one can go back to the challenges and deal with them on a more even keel.

Second, for the couple to feel the special preciousness of stepfamily living, they must realize that stepfamilies require a different kind of parenting. *The biological parent whether it is the woman or the man needs to be the primary disciplinarian.* On the other hand, the nonbiological parent, whether it is the woman or the man, needs to be the secondary supportive disciplinarian.

If the stepparent is the man and the biological parent is the woman, their previous roles may need to be reversed. The woman as the biological parent needs to be the primary disciplinarian. As the nonbiological parent the man needs to be more like an aunt or an uncle providing mentoring and being the supportive disciplinarian. This reverse from previous roles may be difficult to accept. Often this change can result in the couple feeling inept. The male stepparent who is nonbiological may feel that stepfamily living is illogical. The woman who is the biological parent may experience her new role as not being apparent.

As the stepparent, the man may naturally feel the need to be the primary disciplinarian. As a result, stress can ripple throughout the family. It has been said that if you grip a golf club the way it feels the most uncomfortable, it will be right. Initially most people may want to grab the club in the palm of the right hand where it feels more natural to give a feeling of control. But this grip creates too much tension, which restricts clubhead speed and can send the ball hooking sharply to the left.

The nonbiological parent taking a different parenting role may be very uncomfortable. It can be said of stepparenting, "One needs to parent the way it feels most uncomfortable for it to be right." There is certainly some truth in this statement if one does not swallow it whole.

There generally is a certain sense of awkwardness and a feeling of inadequacy for the biological woman to become the primary disciplinarian. There can be a feeling that the nonbiological male is falling down on the job, taking the secondary position. The woman can realize that she can change her parenting style and step up to the plate with serenity, courage, and wisdom and be the disciplinarian that is required. She can reverse her previous role within her own personality style. She does not have to become a different person. For the woman to reverse her role, she will need to become bold. It certainly will take much courage to help the woman not to become discouraged.

The option of not adapting can create havoc. If the nonbiological male follows through with his mistaken feeling that it is his obligation to be the leader in discipline, the child may withdraw or rebel, sending shock waves throughout the family. The stepfather may become angry that the child is not obeying. Then the mother can feel that the father is too hard on the child, creating a rift between the couple. The couple then can become adrift.

The stepfather then may feel unappreciated. As a result, he may feel being on the fringes of family living. To make matters more difficult, the stepparent may feel the brunt of the anger of the children regarding their losses, particularly the loss of time that they previously had with one of their biological parents.

Thus, it is important for a male nonbiological parent to be more of a mentor. He needs to grip the family more lightly with less tension. If the male nonbiological parent grips the stepfamily with tension, the results that would occur may be hard to mention. Being the primary disciplinarian can feel like intrusive meddling to the child. It works best when his role is closer to a mentor or an uncle. Instant love does not happen. Bonding does take time. Spending some one-to-one time with the stepchild can help create a more comfortable relationship. It is important to be with the stepchildren and have enjoyable times where no issues are being discussed.

If the relationship is built solely on dealing with disciplinary issues, solid bonding may be on shaky ground. Like the golf swing being out of control with too much tension, the family then becomes out of control with too much strife. What began to feel natural in striving to make the family function harmoniously often brings chaos.

Consequently, if the nonbiological parent becomes the primary disciplinarian and grips the family too tightly, the stepfamily may veer out of control. The power struggles with the children may become overpowering. Increasing tension can result, creating reactive, escalating conflict without resolution. The stepfamily faces a learning curve to get off the hook. They need to be hooked on healthy stepfamily living.

In golf, it is more effective to place the club in the fingers of the right hand and diagonally across the left hand. This grip creates more freedom of movement in the wrist to give more power, control, and more consistency in the swing. It creates less tension in the rest of the body, allowing the muscles to move faster and more smoothly.

Instead of hooking the ball sharply to the left, the ball will go much straighter. As a result, the golfer can become hooked on the more functional grip. When the nonbiological male experiences that a more relaxed approach is more effective, he can become hooked on changing roles to promote healthy, less chaotic tension.

When the biological mother accepts her role as primary disciplinarian, the parenting partnership will help the stepfamily to be in step. Losses always produce some gains. Dealing with the losses can help the stepfamily experience the gains of the precious uniqueness of stepfamily living.

Stepfamilies: Where Do I Fit In?

Everyone needs to feel like they belong and have a place.
In stepfamily living, one can feel like they are displaced.

It is awkward for stepparents, as they do not have a clear role.
They may feel they are striving to put a square peg into a round hole.

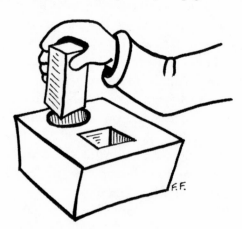

They have the challenge of giving respect to the existing family relationships and also of becoming a part of the family. Their responsibilities are often not clearly defined. Stepparents may err on two extremes. On the one hand, they may lose themselves as they simply take on the colors of the family like a chameleon. They lose themselves as they accommodate the wishes of the family.

On the other hand, they may become controlling, striving to change the family to their own wishes. In this effort, they are not rubber-stamping the wishes of the family. They may be stomping on the family's stomping grounds, striving to shape it to be similar to their familiar old stomping grounds. The stepparent wants to feel at home to be their best. But as this parent feels displaced, they may feel a sense of unrest. They may even feel like an unwelcomed guest. To feel that they have their own place is their quest; they are striving to find some resemblance of their old nest.

Then, there is the third more healthy choice. The needs of all the family members are taken into account as the family evolves into a new form. There can be a metamorphosis. The family members that once felt like they were imprisoned in a cocoon and had no control or influence can turn into butterflies. Then, they will have the freedom to help the family to fly beautifully in formation.

In reality, listening to each other can be overwhelmingly difficult. Each person in the family may be going through many internal struggles. This inner stress may result in so much inner pain that it makes into a huge challenge to empathize with the plight of their partner, child, or stepchild.

Many years ago, I had a tooth pulled and decided not to cancel the afternoon counseling appointment. I found myself in so much pain that my counseling became lame. I had to be honest and tell the counselee that my physical pain was crippling my ability to help her with her emotional pain and complex situations. I rescheduled the session. The next session went better as the pain had dissipated, and I was able to attend to what was happening in her life and worked with her to develop strategies to strengthen her coping skills. It is significant that each family member finds creative ways to reduce their inner stress and pain. Then they can become empowered to attend to what other family members are experiencing.

The noncustodial parents may feel guilty for not being able to see their children. When they do see the children, this guilt may create overcompensation in time and money. They are trying to make up for lost time. This guilt may make it difficult for them to see the biological parent's point of view. The noncustodial parent may easily become defensive from the biological parent's criticism. Noncustodial parents may feel like they are in a dilemma as they ponder the awesome challenges; it may leave them with a tremor. They certainly need courage to steady their hands in the midst of what can seem like impossible demands.

Noncustodial parents who spend part-time with their children may feel guilty about spending more time with their stepchildren. They may feel guilty about rearing someone else's child and spending less time parenting their own. Also, they may have difficulty in dealing with the pain of having to say good-bye to their own children as they return to the custodial parent. This pain can contribute to their spending less and less time with their own children. Then tension can develop with their ex-spouses who resent having to deal with what they feel is an irresponsible father.

Custodial parents may feel that they are left holding the bag in parenting without much support. What their children are losing in the process may be painful. The custodial parent has to deal with the reaction of the children regarding their anger in not being able to see their noncustodial parent as often.

To fit in, stepparents want to have recognition from their stepchildren. With the internal feelings of the stepchildren, often, appreciation is not in the cards. Positive feelings do not instantly occur. Thus, stepparents feel that their efforts are taken for granted. They do not feel that they make a worthwhile difference in family living. Their dilemma may seem like a no-win situation. Instead of fitting in, the stepparents may feel like having a fit.

They may feel aggravated along with feeling exploited. These uncomfortable feelings may result when their stepchildren say they do not do things as well as their biological parents. The children may play one against the other. The playground can become transformed from a field of dreams into a field of battle.

The stepparent then needs strong support from the biological parent. Empathy can help the stepparent to adjust. A foundation can be built for the stepparent to become a successful mate and stepparent. It is a monumental task for each family member to adjust. Quality time is needed for the family to build trust. The stepparent needs a welcome mat of understanding. Then, gradually, they can find their place and have a happy landing.

Stepfamilies: Coping as a Couple

A good marriage can become the stepfamily's carriage.

In a traditional family, building a strong marriage is challenging. A couple engaging in the complexity of stepfamily living can feel overwhelmed.

Issues such as child support, alimony, shared parenthood, telephone calls, Father's Day, Mother's Day—all remind that one of both partners had a love relationship with someone else. Even a child can have features and behaviors that remind one of the failed relationship. Stepfamily living can produce a huge learning curve. Being a good student will keep the family from a damaging swerve.

Even though *ex* means that the relationship is over, in stepfamily living, the relationship is not over. A residue of psychological attachment of mixed feelings of love and anger may still be alive. Children may create a need to connect with their former mate regarding parenting issues. Past feelings can surface with the connection, and these feelings can interfere in the present marriage. Also, they can impede the parenting challenge.

Former losses and breaches of trust can infiltrate communication with the present mate. It may become more difficult to risk sharing vulnerable feelings. Handling conflictive issues may become more challenging. Feelings surfacing may be acted out on the present mate. On the other hand, trust can be built overtime with mutual respect. Gradually, the foundation can be built for stepfamily living.

One cardinal truth is that the best gift you can give to your children is a good marriage. A stepfamily's marriage can become the children's carriage. The strength of the couple's relationship is the key to stability. This key unlocks and untangles the thorny issues that typically emerge. If the foundation is shaky, stepfamily issues can crumble the structure of the family. Each member may feel like they are just receiving crumbs. Their experience may feel crummy.

It is evident that the marriage relationship must not become lost in the midst of dealing with stepfamily issues. Time must be set aside to nurture this relationship. With a strong marriage, the children can receive sunshine that they need to grow. The parents will have a sunnier disposition. The stable marriage's carriage can carry the family to fulfilling stepfamily living.

Boundaries and choices need to be made to give the marriage the priority that it deserves. Then, the chaos and confusion will gradually move to cooperation and clarity. While stepfamily living may never become neat and tidy, it can become a fulfilling experience.

Issues can be confronted with more mutual respect. Here is an example of a nonsupportive and supportive response to a stepparent's comment.

Spouse 1:   I am going to take the kids to Grandmother's this weekend.

Spouse 2: What do you mean you want to take your kids to see their grandmother? We haven't been anywhere alone since we got married.

A nonsupportive response could be this:

Spouse 1: You knew before we got married that my kids and I were close to their grandmother.

Respecting the frustrations that surface in conflictive needs
Can turn defensive, detrimental reactions to good deeds.

A supportive response could be:

Spouse 1: You are right. We really have not nurtured our relationship. What would you like to do?
Spouse 2: I think it would be great if the two of us could go to the beach for the weekend. What about Grandmother taking care of the children?
Spouse 1: Sounds like a win-win to me.

This couple was able to listen to each other and problem solve to meet the needs of the marriage. Openness to the frustrations of the spouse is the key to problem solving. Defensiveness is the culprit as it becomes the catalyst for escalating, reactive conflicts, resolving nothing.

Mutual respect can greatly enhance communication. They then can remain united and can cope successfully with stepfamily issues. Then each family member can feel that they come out okay as their needs are addressed in a reputable manner.

Stepfamilies: Creating Healthy Stepchildren

Stepfamilies can positively affect the next generation.
They can leave a legacy worthy of veneration.

Providing a healthy soil in which stepchildren can grow is a huge challenge for our society. The health of the next generation is dependent upon this endeavor. Stepfamilies, to be a fertile ground for stepchildren, must provide leadership and healing. They themselves need a coach as a mentor to prevent stepfamilies from being filled with rancor.

A part of this process concerns helping them with anger. They had no choice in the matter of divorce or death. Anger may then spill over in the mix of family living. They often have anger over the biological parent for the loss. That may be anger at the custodial parent for having to move.

Moreover, they may be angry at having to adjust to a stepparent who is not their real parent. If they are teenagers with many internal changes, the adjustment challenges may be even greater. This is a stage where they are putting on their wings regarding dealing with authority. This stage can be crucial as they later embark upon the real world. In stepfamilies, the authority issue becomes more complicated and challenging.

For the children to have a healthy climate, the children need to have permission to have a relationship with their other parent without the custodial parent's interference. Putting them into a loyalty dilemma can stunt their emotional growth. By having sustained positive connections with both parents, children can gradually let go of guilty feelings.

Another feeling that can fester in the stepchild is fear. If conflict emerges in the complexities of stepfamily living, the child may fear that another family is going to come apart. If the parents immerse themselves in juggling jobs and a new spouse, children may question the parents' love. Juggling too many balls may result in the parents dropping the ball in the parenting challenge.

Fear may surface as the child leaves the familiar and faces the unknown. As they experience fear and confusion, they may express these feelings through misbehavior. The stress that the family is experiencing may make it difficult for the parents to choose their battles. Consequently, they may overreact, causing the problems to escalate.

They may create too many battles. Children need limits and discipline, but they also need a place to honestly say what life is like for them. Then their feelings will not spill over into an already-complex environment and create an overwhelming flood of stressful reactions.

Stepfamilies' children face many formidable changes. The losses and additions create a ruggedness of difficult, vast ranges.

Having a brainstorming session with the whole family where all suggestions are respected and considered can help each person to feel that they matter. The aspects of stepfamily living can be dealt with in a more constructive way. The family putting the puzzle together can resolve their feeling puzzled. These pieces can fall into place as the family no longer feels muzzled.

Also, activities that give a family a respite from the adjustment challenges can be enriching. Then, stepping into stepfamily living can become more harmonious. Opening up the package of stepfamily living does not have to be like opening up a Pandora's box of misery. It can be filled with unique gifts to enhance one's life. By having the serenity to accept what they cannot change and the courage to change what they should change, healthy adjustments can be made. Stepfamilies can be in step.

Wisdom

> Stepparenting is wise when both partners adjust,
> And their roles produce growth in the family and trust.

Courage

> Stepparenting is courageous when they hit bumps and ride out
>   of the trials,
> And the tires in the family will last many miles.

Serenity

> Stepfamilies are serene when they listen to each other;
> Then they can live in harmony and not be a bother.

The following guiding questions are adapted to the chapter on stepparenting. These thought-provoking questions are to help you ponder personal applications and the Serenity Prayer. The resulting soul-searching exercise can aid you in more fully experiencing the Serenity Prayer lifestyle as you apply this prayer to all aspects of your daily life.

These questions embodied in the Serenity Prayer then can begin a personal lifelong quest in becoming more skillful in living the Serenity Prayer lifestyle. Then the Serenity Prayer can become increasingly embedded in your life. The prayer can help smooth out the edges of life and prevent your lifestyle from becoming coarse. The voice of your life will not become hoarse. The Serenity Prayer then is a great spiritual resource to help you keep the course.

Coaching Questions: Personally Applying the Serenity Prayer in Stepfamily Living

Remember:

You are not starting from scratch. You have long since been hatched. In your life, your efforts have not gone for naught. You can be commended for what you have already wrought.

These questions and thoughts are for the purpose of serving as a personal guiding coach. They can give you the opportunity to prayerfully brainstorm. Then the challenges and solutions in your particular situation can surface. You may find opportunities to build upon what you are already doing well and take another step forward.

Engaging the Serenity Prayer with the issue of stepfamily living can become a profitable soul-searching pilgrimage. In the process, you will be honing skills that will enable you to apply the prayer to all aspects of your life.

1. What do you need to accept that is unchangeable regarding stepfamily living?

"Lord, help me accept what I cannot change regarding stepfamily living." It is very difficult to let go of the unalterable aspects of life. They can bring you to the altar when you falter in reducing our internal strife. For example, one cannot change all the losses each family member has experienced and all of the adaptations that need to be made.

2. What do you need to change that you can change regarding stepfamily living?

"Lord, help me to change the things I need to change regarding stepfamily living."

You can make a difference that counts. The worthless behaviors, we will renounce. For example, listening to others' needs can help the stepfamily to gain a sense of the changes that one needs to make regarding the adjustments of stepfamily living.

3. What are some things you are changing in the wrong manner concerning stepfamily living?

"Lord, help me to stop the manners that I need to change concerning stepfamily living."

Does the end justify the means?

Is the process worthy of the progress?

Does the manner of change have good manners?

It can help by thinking of an example concerning what you have changed in a good manner. Begin with a positive feeling.

When one changes things in the wrong way, there is no serenity. There will likely only be enmity. For example, the nonbiological parent, particularly the male, may try to be the primary disciplinarian.

4. What are you striving to change that you should not be trying to modify regarding stepfamily living?

"Lord, help me to stop striving to change aspects of stepfamily living that I should not change."
To be nosy can become very noisy. Trying to make improvements may be in the best of intentions. These efforts can result in futile dissensions. For example, in stepfamily living, it may be hard to sit back and let others take the lead when you would do it a different way. Combining two families that are different can put one out of their comfort zone into a big learning curve.

5. What are some things that you do not know whether they are changeable or not changeable regarding stepfamily living?

"Lord, give me the wisdom to know what is changeable and unchangeable regarding stepfamily living."
There are times when the decision is not clear whether something can be changed that is so dear. This takes a time of prayer to stop and explore to make decisions that one will not deplore. For example, one needs to give

the family time to adapt to see what the best form it needs to take. If one has a preconceived notion, one can create much commotion. With wisdom, the family can be in tune with each other to see what needs to be accepted. Then one can have the energy to put on other more pertinent challenges.

6. **How can the powerful dynamics of serenity, wisdom, and courage help you in moving toward a healthier stepfamily living?**

"Lord, grant me the strength to fully utilize serenity, wisdom, and courage in growing a healthier stepfamily living?"

The Serenity Prayer gives us meaning and purpose
And helps us to live life filled with an overflowing surplus.

Imagine what you would look, feel, and act like if you were filled with wisdom regarding stepfamily living.

Visualize what you would look, feel, and act like if you were filled with courage regarding stepfamily living.

Envision what you would look, feel, and act like if you were filled with serenity regarding stepfamily living.

In each state of mind regarding stepfamily living, how would your body language appear?

What would be your facial expression?

How would you look out of your eyes?

What would the tone of your voice sound like?

What more would you be accomplishing?

How would you envision people responding to you differently?

How would you project your life to be different today, in one week, in one month, in one year, in five years . . . ? Your life would be different indeed.

Cultivate these feelings. Develop a vision, and it will turn into a mission—a mission statement that is empowered. You can apply a vision and a mission to the vast array of your present and future challenges. The Serenity Prayer can serve as fission to spark the energy to carry out the plan.

7. What do I need to change behaviorally regarding stepfamily living?

"Lord, help me to make the behavioral changes that I need to make regarding stepfamily living."

You need to affirm what you are doing well. Owning these strengths can help you feel swell. You can then take the next step with inspiration. Then this step of growth will not be out of desperation. One can begin to row with the flow and experience life's progressive journey with a glow. For example, one may need to change who is the primary disciplinarian. The biological parent needs to be the primary disciplinarian.

8. What do I need to change regarding my feelings and attitudes about stepfamily living?

"Lord, help me to change my feelings and attitudes that I need to change regarding stepfamily living."

One's attitude is one's life's outlook. If it is negative, it can lead to a donnybrook. If it is positive, it can provide one a life's stance to celebrate each day with the feeling of wanting to dance. For example, one needs to change the attitude that the family is going to be like a regular family. Stepfamilies have unique common challenges.

Part 3

The Serenity Prayer: A Coach for Healing Inner Turmoil

Chapter 6

Healing Grief with Courage and Wisdom

Your grief must not be held captive.
It must be allowed to be active.

Grief must be free to take its natural course,
Or it will try to bust free by sheer force.

The Serenity Prayer raises these issues regarding grief. You need to know what to strive to change, how to change what you should change, what not to attempt to change, and what you cannot change. Growing in understanding and accomplishing these tasks in grief work certainly takes serenity, wisdom, and courage.

Engaging the Serenity Prayer with the issue of bereavement can become a profitable soul-searching pilgrimage. The questions at the end of the chapter help you to ponder and apply the issues that this chapter raises. In the process, you will be honing skills that will enable you to apply the prayer to all aspects of your life.

If we do not honor the loss,
Grief can create havoc as the loss can be a domineering, ruthless
boss.

Grieving is letting go of a loss that is unchangeable. The person in mourning then can gradually place energies on what they can change.

Then, by reordering one's life, one can gradually experience the dawning of a new day of serenity. Painful grief work takes courage. Wisdom is necessary to navigate its waters without drowning in the tears. Using the waters of the tears as buoyancy can provide healing and hope. The resulting serenity is needed to move toward the future with clarity.

To begin on a lighter but serious note, I will share two of my first encounters with grief as a child. When I was eight years old, I spent many hours making a kite. I acquired the sticks from a tree. Next, I made a crossbar and tied the two pieces together. Paper trash bags were utilized to cover the sticks in the shape of a kite. Old sheets were found to make a tail. I was quite proud of my creation.

It was time to see if the kite would fly. To my amazement, the kite caught the wind in my backyard and soared to heights that I never would have dreamed. The performance of the kite as it became airborne thrilled my heart, and I was as high as a kite. The kite flourished flying across the sky. It had come to life. This creation playing in the sky was fashioned and birthed by my own hands.

Then something dreadful happened that was completely out of my control. The kite rose high above a large pecan tree. The wind began to die down, and the kite began its downward descent toward its slow, agonizing death. The top of the pecan tree became its prison as it was hopelessly snagged. The tail would never again ascend into the beautiful, bright blue sky. As the months and years went by, the only evidence of the kite's ill-fated flight was its tail flapping helplessly in the wind.

When I was eleven years old, I had a parakeet. Often I would take the beautiful green-and-yellow bird out of the cage and play with him. He loved to peck on an apple. On one occasion, the parakeet was out of the cage, pecking on an apple. I was not aware that the door was open as our house was being renovated.

The parakeet saw its chance and flew into the top of that same pecan tree near the kite's tail. Unlike the kite, the parakeet flew away and disappeared. His happy chirping sounds were silenced. He had no idea that death was imminent. The beautiful green-and-yellow bird had no skills to make it on its own.

I learned what it means to experience loss. These losses were the beginning of many losses that I miss. I began to learn that much is out of my control that I must not resist. Trying to hold on to what is gone will restrict one's future life. Instead of moving on, one will experience chronic strife. It is important to let go of what one cannot change. This surrender makes it possible for the loss to expand life's range.

Many years later as an adult, I went by the old homeplace to find to my dismay that the tree had been cut down. Now there was not a trace of the life of the kite left. My heart temporarily sunk. I got into a temporary funk. It may have been at this point that I completed my good-bye.

Of course, I have had many much tougher losses, but smaller losses can begin to help cope with larger ones. At the same time, one cannot be completely prepared for a significant loss. Losses come in different packages.

The presenting issues have commonalities but are unique to the individual person.

In grief, we face one of our most painful limitations. We know that we cannot bring them back into our lives. It can be extraordinarily difficult to grieve and let them go. By gradually letting them go, the slow, arduous process of the grief journey can begin. The grief journey is not brief. It is a slow movement where one feels that their ship has hit a reef. It is difficult to say good-bye, as the tears begin to flow and one begins to cry.

As we say good-bye, we will gradually become free to move into the future. Increasing energy can be placed into reordering one's life. Then we can move on toward changing what we can. In our journey, the Serenity Prayer will be much in demand.

Grief is a journey of healing toward acceptance. Mourning is asking God to help us to let go and to accept what we cannot change. One may never be able to completely accept the loss. On the other hand, one can heal sufficiently to gradually experience more freedom from being preoccupied by the loss. Then, one can become more occupied in the present and spend more time planning for the future. Memories can progressively become more pleasant than painful. Gradually, the memories that brought a flood of grief will now bring solace and relief.

Death is woven into the very fabric of life. When a loved one dies, this fabric is ripped open. In the old days, quilts were patched together with scraps of cloth. No quilt was exactly alike. Experiencing grief can be like a quilt that has a section ripped out and discarded. This patch is lost and can never be replaced. The quilt loses its former identity. The gaping hole leaves a grieving gap. One may feel that they received a bum rap. Someone with skillful hands can mend the quilt with another patch. This quilt can still be filled with a different color that will match.

One can grieve the lost person, but nothing can replace the person. One can reorder their lives to adjust to the loss. With much grief work, one can come to terms with their loss. One can redesign the quilt, and life can still be filled with beauty and color. A spiritual connection can then be felt that makes one's heart feel warm and melt.

To navigate the deep waters of grief is a formidable task. Sometimes it may feel like one is drowning in their flood of tears. The challenge is to use the healing buoyancy of these tears to keep one afloat. Then, it will be possible to swim to the other side of the grief and forge a new life without the loved one. The sun can peep preciously above the horizon, creating the dawning of a new day. The Serenity Prayer of acceptance is what we pray.

It takes courage to do grief work, as it can be a painful, confusing, and lonely time. The emotions of grief can become an up-and-down experience. This roller-coaster ride can be disturbing and perplexing. Many well-meaning people will try to give the grieving person a quick fix. Some people may say, "When are you going to get over it?"

The wounds make one's life feel like a wreck, and the lost blood feels like more than a speck.

When I was going through a divorce many years ago, I visited my brother in California for eight days. On the way back, I felt so good that I thought I was healed. The next few days, I went through deeper grief than I had experienced before. Working through grief requires much energy. The time in California had given me the reserve of energy to grieve more deeply.

Our culture does much to stifle and squelch the expression of grief. When one drives without a functioning muffler, one will receive a ticket. When one does not muffle their grief, society can give the grieving person a warning ticket of shame. This warning ticket communicates to one not to grieve again.

When I was a ten years old, I saw a movie that depicted the Spartan army. In one scene, a huge man was dressed up in his striking armor. His helmet, armor, and sword contained steel mixed with a rich purple color. The soldier looked formidable and striking.

At his side was his eight-year-old son who was all dressed up in military garb just like his dad. In one sense, it was cute. In another sense, it was very sad. The father took out his sharp sword and sliced a huge gushing gash in his son's right arm. He then looked at his son and said, "Now, that didn't hurt, did it?" The son grimaced and muffled his pain and said, "No, Daddy, it did not hurt."

Our society tends to minimize the deep pain of grief. We may say, "Get over it. It did not hurt that much." Thus, many Americans have learned not to let their tears give voice to the pain. It is like they lost their freedom of speech when it comes to grief. They feel that the freedom that we enjoy as Americans does not include grieving.

The impact of the loss is kept in the dark, and the emotions of grief become toxic to the soul. Like germs spreading the infection of a wound, the stifled grief emotions can play havoc upon grieving people's emotional and physical health. The abscess is not lanced, and the journey toward healing has not yet begun.

The good news is that a person may grow toward healing. While no one would choose grief, facing it can help a person to grow creatively in ways that he/she would not have grown without this experience. Grief then needs to address both the promise and the pain. Then the grief work will become a part of recovery's gain.

When I was a chaplain for people with developmental disabilities, I was asked to visit a group's home to help a resident to deal with his father's death. He and four of his friends were in the room where we gathered. I asked one of his friends to go out the door. Next, I asked him to come back in. Then I told the resident that his father went through the door and will not be coming back. His friends each one came up to him and gave him a hug. He was able to grieve with support. There can be such a process as "good grief."

Grieving as a Family

> Families need to give each member the right to grieve
> Each member needs to let go as well as have a reprieve.

Families that pray together stay together. This can be said of grief. Families that grieve together stay together. It is important for families to cope well so that they will be equal to the challenge.

Families that are disconnected when faced with grief have a particular challenge in sharing their grief and supporting each other. They tend to keep the grief to themselves. Some have a message that sad feelings are bad and are not to be felt, much less expressed. Grief can be a time that self-esteem is low.

This unresolved loss will leave its mud tracks on the family system. Grief is designed to be dealt with as a family. The coping strength is stronger. Healing can take place. Then, pure tracks of love and compassion can touch the heart of every family member.

Thus, there needs to be a connection in the midst of grief. Each family member will have different ways of dealing with loss. There must be a sense of togetherness as well as separateness in the grief process to give proper balance. A family that is overly connected may want each family member to grieve alike. There will not be any tolerance for variations.

This rigidity can place too much pressure on family members that have varying needs for privacy and connection. In this overly connected family, one family member will assume that he/she knows exactly what others are feeling and may not listen to the unique experiences of the other.

Simple connections can be made by hugs. A sense of closeness can be made with touch or words. Some family members may need more hugs while others may need more words. More silence may be in order for some in bereavement. But virtually all family members need some proportion of all three. Each family member needs to honor the loss by permitting grief. Expressions of grief can be unique, but no significant grief is brief. Understanding each family member's needs can enable the family to give supportive mourning deeds.

There has been little written concerning how loss affects a family. Most of the literature has expressed how it affects individuals. But one must realize that the loss of a family member ripples throughout the family system. Education can help one not to be hit blindsided in the midst of the grieving process.

Some families try to go on like nothing has happened, and then the effects of grief disrupts family living. It is a flood of grief that hits the family by surprise. This torrent may place emotions at an overwhelming level. The undertow of pent-up grief may take one out into deeper waters. Then it will become more difficult to swim back to shore to reorder one's life.

Thus, the family needs to have open communication about the death. The loss must be discussed and clarified. Feelings about the loss need to be expressed. A family can grow creatively through grief with wisdom and courage. The family in its own unique manner needs to share their mourning experience. Then their mornings will become less painful. It helps in this process to share memories. This sharing emphasizes how important the family member was to them. Then there is a reason to acknowledge the pain. The pain is an expression of the important part of their lives that they have lost.

They then can have their mourning rituals that can allow grief to have its say without crashing down on them. Consequently, grief will be permitted. The tears will not be pent-up and have to wait until the pressure of grief is so great that it knocks the floodgates down.

As the family moves through the grief process, reorganization can take place. Healing can enable the family to gradually adjust to the loss. This includes reviving the emotional stability of the family. Also, structural changes in tasks, responsibilities, and roles may need to be made. Many times one person will be the caretaker for the family in terms of tending to details and other emotions. It is important that this person have their own support and time alone to grieve. Otherwise, the caretaker can experience an avalanche of the emotions of others.

Grief is a part of life. Families can live and grow through the resulting challenges. This journey will inevitably have bumps on the road. But slowly the bumps will lessen as families reach out for help within the family and inside the community. With support, the family can come to terms with the loss and can experience warm goose bumps of compassion.

It is unrealistic to say that one will completely heal from a significant loss. Healthy healing can be the bridge for the family to cross the most troubling aspects of grief. Then family members can move forward to the future.

How the Death of a Child Can Challenge a Marriage

The agony of the death of their child can leave a couple in
overwhelming sorrow.
They cannot go to a bank and get a loan of love to borrow.

They are in debt with absorbing tears and pain.
They can be at a loss to give to their partner while emotionally
lame.

The marriage vows state that one takes one's mate for better or for worse. Losing a child is one of the most difficult challenges a marriage can face. This crisis can cut away at the very fiber of a relationship. It can leave a relationship frayed, or it can leave it in shambles. Some couples are able to survive the test and grow through this difficult time. It helps for the family to be aware of both the obstacles and possible solutions.

It takes much skill for a marriage to survive such a blow. Each partner is so stunned and shocked by the loss that they may have little to give to each other. A marriage relationship stays alive and grows through giving and receiving. This crisis upsets the balance. Both partners are going through a crisis at the same time. The grief is so deep that each partner may turn inside. When one has a toothache, one is thinking about oneself. This is an extraordinarily, painful heartache that cannot experience relief by quickly being extracted.

In fact, it is so painful that the numbness and shock may last longer than normal grief. It becomes difficult to share feelings of love to one's mate. The feelings of grief can be like a volcano that has erupted. The normal pattern of their lives has been disrupted. The couple has the challenge of facing the agonizing molten rock to begin the journey of healing from the devastating shock. The challenge is to reorder one's life to gradually feel as solid as a rock.

One of the dangers concerns the different ways that the husband and wife grieve. The differences in the way partners grieve may create tension and misunderstanding that only makes a very complicated recovery more problematic.

Men tend to become caught up in work as a way to cope with grief. They have a need to do something after a loss. Women need to talk about it. They need to share the story many times to move toward healing. Because the man is more reserved than the woman is and tends to get back on his routine quicker, the woman may think that he is uncaring.

Husbands often are not able to understand the wives' intense emotions, and they may wonder why she cannot get it behind her. Thus, friction arises. The partners need to know that there is not only one way to grieve. No timetable should be set. However, if one becomes stuck and depression sets in, professional help may be needed.

The marriage needs to find a way to stay afloat in the turbulent waters of grieving from losing a child. Some skillful, sensitive way of supporting each other can provide a life preserver to help the marriage from drowning. The angry stage of grief may be especially challenging. One partner may use the other partner as a shock absorber for their grief. The other partner may act in their anger and become depressed. This pattern can weaken the relationship.

One partner may become defensive, striving to protect oneself from the attacks. One spouse may be attacking, striving to deal with their anger. During grief, the marriage relationship is not business as usual. It takes patience to wait for their relationship to again become musical. The pain prevents the music from being upbeat. The sad, symphonic sound releases tears of healing that grievers seek.

To meet the challenge, each partner needs to realize when they are acting out their grief. Then they can find support from a friend or counselor. Each partner needs to fill up their own cup. Then spouses will gradually be able to become more supportive to each other.

The Funeral and the Grief Process

Funeral rituals are to help one to begin to say good-bye.
They allow the opportunity for people to begin to cry.

This important ritual allows the reality of the death to seep in,
And the slow grief process can begin.

Funerals planned and carried out authentically and effectively can fan the flames of grief and let the burning pain of grief be felt. Then, support can be given to comfort the family. Keeping that balance of pain and comfort can help the bereaved to begin to heal and cleanse their souls.

The funeral service can give people an opportunity to express thoughts and feelings about the deceased. They need to share both positive and negative feelings. There is a tendency to overidealize and overeulogize a person at a funeral. It is difficult to share negative feelings in the cooperate ritual of a funeral, but a person needs to express what they will miss as well as what they will not miss.

The sensitive pastor, family, or friend may give the person permission to share these negative feelings as a part of the care of the bereaved. The competent counselor must also give a climate so all feelings are given their due respect. These feelings include the joy and the pain, the love and the anger, and the security and the fear.

The funeral should be an authentic reflection of the deceased person. Creative ways can be developed for people to tell anecdotes to bring the memories alive. Pointing out accomplishments can help bring pride to the family. The departed loved one's life had meaning and purpose. Also, in the midst of the pride, the memories can help begin flushing the grief from the heart.

The funeral service provides a catalyst for a network of community support. This network can help to strengthen the person for the grief tasks. The funeral sets the foundation for other kinds of help such as a support group. These people especially need support to let grief run its natural course. While the funeral ritual is significant, it is just a step in the long journey of grief. Usually, the first year is the toughest. During this time, grief may feel like it is consuming one's life.

If grief is running its normal course, the preoccupation with the death of the loved one will begin to slowly subside. The griever can gradually become more occupied by memories of the person's life. These memories can bring inspiration instead of desperation. Then the person in mourning will have more energy to move forward with their own life. They will have a reason to get up in the morning.

The funeral then is an important part of grief taking its normal course. The person needs to spend time to view the body. One is in shock, especially if it was a sudden death. Lingering with the body helps one facing the reality of the death. One must have the reality of the death to pierce the barricade around the heart that says, "It is not true." The funeral can play a significant part of facing the reality of the death and of beginning to say, "Good-bye."

If a person continues to linger and leaving seems to be overwhelming, it may be a sign of having extreme difficulty in facing the reality of the death. This difficulty in leaving may be a sign of being stuck in striving to hold on to the person's life. One then especially needs compassionate guidance.

Consequently, having the funeral can touch hearts in many ways with the reality of the finality of death. It can also create a foundation for meaningful memories, helping one to move forward into the future. These thoughts can keep the warm memories of the person's life intact without the flames overheating. The eternal flames then can warm the heart instead of parching the soul.

A Tragic Death Tries One's Soul

A disastrous death makes the tugboat's challenge great.
To take the boat ashore, the tugboat must tow extra weight.
The tears of the passengers have loaded the ship,
Which makes it seem like shore is an impossible trip.

Others have given hope by making it to shore.
They give inspiration, and hope grows more and more.
The shore becomes sighted; they see the land.
Hope helps the grievers to begin to take command.

The death has tugged at one's soul in anguish.
The tugboat did not allow one to continuously languish.
You were able to move through the valley.
As a result, your life began to rally.

When the death of a family member occurs suddenly and tragically, the grief challenge is greatly inflated. When the bubble bursts, the explosion of grief is much more intense and confusing. A life is stolen suddenly without warning. The cruel fate allows no time to say good-bye.

The shock waves become like an earthquake, which jolts the family. Cracks can be left creating a chasm between family members, complicating family living. Tremors may be felt for months and years to come. The landscape of one's world will look and feel different. This emotional earthquake can create cracks in one's faith. There are no neat answers from God, but there is his loving presence.

It is natural to question God during a time of grief. It may seem like prayers have not been answered, and there is no relief. Well-meaning people strive to give answers as to why in an effort to divert attention away from the challenge of one's facing the painful, grieving good-bye. Comfort comes with another's compassionate presence. This presence reminds one that God, who seemed so far away, is still at the griever's residence.

A tragedy accentuates the process of grief. Shock may become more overwhelming. Emotional pain may become deeper, and physical symptoms may be more severe. It is not unusual for grief to have many of the same symptoms as clinical depression. There may be appetite changes, sleep disturbances, physical complaints, decreased sexual desire, loss of energy, inability to concentrate, and a need to withdraw.

You may not need professional help if you are gradually healing. On the other hand, if you become stuck in grief or the pain becomes too difficult to bear, then finding a therapist who understands grieving can help heal the cracks in your faith and family.

If you have had emotional problems or family problems prior to a tragic death, it is highly likely that professional counseling will be necessary to help you grow toward emotional and spiritual health. You would rather gain serenity than have great wealth. You could easily slip into a clinical depression and could need professional help.

There is no time frame for grieving. One never completely heals from any death, much less a tragic death. Grief can surface with strong emotion for some time. As you heal, the grief lessens, and the painful loss gradually moves in to the background. It is important for you to be growing at your own pace and to continue to reorder your life after the loss. You deserve help in this process, whether it is community support or professional help or both. You can gradually come back into the land of the living because others have been so understanding and giving.

A tragedy definitely tries the soul, but you can cope and deal creatively with the monumental misfortune. Monuments of tribute in a variety of creative forms can promote healing and hope. The trial can create a change in you that can broaden your horizon regarding the human plight. You may eventually find ways to utilize this learning in helping others cope with a sudden, unexpected tragedy in their lives. The soul may be severely tried, but it can survive and eventually thrive.

Disenfranchised Grief: Grief with No Entitlement

Some unique circumstances give grief a muzzle. Why the community cannot give permission to grieve can be a puzzle. They do not understand that grief needs to be respected and is real. The public will not respond to the griever's appeal.

In recent years, disenfranchised grief has been used to refer to grief that has no permission to express itself. It is chained to the heart and locked. You cannot find the key. The individual's loss is not publicly recognized by others, sometimes not even by themselves. Because the grief cannot be shared, these grievers face special pain and problems. They are facing the burden of hidden sorrow. This grief is voiceless. It has no rights. It cannot stand on its two feet.

We need to own our grief and validate it in order for our grief to stand up and voice its loss. You have certain inalienable rights in America; one is that you have a right to grieve. It is a part of the human experience.

Disenfranchised grief often has no simple answer. One example concerns the death of an ex-husband or ex-wife. The person is not likely to have community support to give permission to grieve. But just because the marriage is over does not mean that there will be no grief. Somehow a voice must be given to the loss. Because of the lack of community support and a lack of understanding, the person may need professional help. The person also needs to nurture one's soul.

A child may lose a pet turtle. The child has a right to be sad and to grieve. But it could become a disenfranchised grief because the family does not understand his need to mourn. The family may say, "It was only a turtle. We will give you another one." They then stifle the feeling that loss brings to the child.

A family whose son or daughter died from AIDS may find that the grief has little right to express itself. People may feel uncomfortable, and the person may grieve in isolation. It may become a complicated grief as normal support may not be available.

Disenfranchised grief may also occur when many people discount the loss of a newborn or a miscarriage with the comment, "It's not as if they knew the child." Yet this ignores the great attachment that forms during pregnancy and the months and years of hoping, dreaming, planning, trying, and waiting. A support group can help as one can experience the understanding and compassion that they deserve.

A person can find it hard to discuss her son's suicide. A parent may be ashamed to mention that her son died trying to commit a robbery. Disenfranchised grievers often lack social support in these circumstances as well.

A family who has a child that is developmentally delayed may experience chronic disenfranchised grief. I once knew a pastor who said he needed two things when the child was born. He needed to celebrate the child that he had and grieve for the normal child that he did not have.

There are different stages when the grief surfaces again and again. A leader in the field of mental retardation who was a very strong man was brought to tears when his child was twenty-one. He remarked, "He will never be able to get married." That is the child he lost. But he has had many joyful moments with the child that he gained.

Grief is real. It needs to be given a voice. It must not remain disenfranchised as it may clog the mind, body, and soul with difficult emotions that need to find their way out to the healing sunshine. Sharing the losses with people who are empathetic can be enormously helpful. Not being able to discuss losses and not being able to feel other's support complicates grief and can be extremely harmful. At best, grief is difficult. When it is not given its due attention, it can become overwhelming.

There are great challenges, but there are some ways to help the grief work to work. If you are a person who has experienced a disenfranchised loss, it must be accepted that wherever there has been attachment, grief will occur. You can have your own private way of grieving. You may go to the cemetery. Journaling often helps. Certain times of the year can be difficult, and you need to find your unique way of grieving and structuring your time to gain distance from the grief. Grief takes much energy. You can escape or overindulge. Escaping means that grief will surface harmfully some time later physically and/or emotionally. Overindulging in grief can prevent you from gradually reordering your life and getting back into the land of the living.

Also, a person who has experienced a major loss needs to give focused time for healing and grieving. The grieving person needs another person who will validate and accept their mourning. Then the grief will not be disenfranchised; it will be embraced with dignity. No matter what the source of grief may be, a person needs to face its reality. Any grief has a right to have its say. One way to help is to pray. Finding a support group of people of like kind can be helpful as you are striving to cope with the loss. You deserve dignity as grief grips your soul. Understanding gives you freedom to grieve to lessen its toll.

Wisdom

Mourning is wise when one gradually comes to terms with grief and begins to reorder their lives as they move into the future.

Courage

The grieving persons are courageous when they are able to endure. The long journey toward healing that may not receive complete cure.

Serenity

Serenity is experienced by the person who is experiencing loss when they have healed enough to come to terms with the cost. A grieving person needs the support of the community to experience more times of serenity. Grief can pull people together. Mourners can gradually see sunshine lighting up the stormy dark weather.

The following guiding questions are adapted to the chapter on grief. These thought-provoking questions are to help you ponder personal applications of the Serenity Prayer. The resulting soul-searching exercise can aid you to more fully experience the Serenity Prayer lifestyle as you apply this prayer to all aspects of your daily life.

These questions embodied in the Serenity Prayer then can begin a personal lifelong quest in becoming more skillful in living the Serenity Prayer lifestyle. Then the Serenity Prayer can become increasingly embedded in your life. The prayer can help smooth out the edges of life and prevent your lifestyle from becoming coarse. The voice of your life will not become hoarse. The Serenity Prayer then is a great spiritual resource to help you keep the course.

Coaching Questions: Applying the Serenity Prayer to the Healing of Grief

Remember:

> You are not starting from scratch.
> You have long since been hatched.
>
> In your life your efforts have not gone for naught.
> You can be commended for what you have already wrought.

These questions and thoughts are for the purpose serving as a personal coaching friend. They can give you the opportunity to prayerfully brainstorm to surface the challenges and solutions in your particular situation.

You may find an opportunity to build upon what you are already doing well and take another step forward. Engaging the Serenity Prayer with the issue of bereavement can become a profitable healing soul-searching pilgrimage.

1. What do you need to accept that you cannot change regarding your loss and grief?

"Lord, grant me the serenity to accept what I cannot change regarding my loss and grief?"

It is very difficult to let go of the unalterable aspects of life. They can bring you to the altar when you falter in reducing your internal strife. For example, you must gradually come to terms with the fact that the significant other is dead. That is not easy. It is a slow journey. Embarking upon a painful and often puzzling grief pilgrimage can find other travelers who understand. This understanding can help the person through the journey to withstand.

2. What do you need to change that you can change regarding your loss and grief?

"Lord, grant me the wisdom to know what I should change regarding my loss and grief?"

One can make a difference that counts, and the worthless behaviors we will renounce. For example, many people have made a difference by having many different kinds of memorials. These creative ways of remembering the deceased by giving a contribution has filled the needs of many people needing help.

3. What are some things you can change that you may be striving to change in the wrong manner regarding your loss and grief?

"Lord, grant me the wisdom to know what I am striving to inappropriately change regarding my loss and grief."

Does the end justify the means?

Is the process worthy of the progress?

Does the manner of change have good manners?

It can help by thinking of an example of what you have changed in a good manner. Begin from a positive feeling.

When one changes matters in the wrong way, there is no serenity. There will likely only be enmity. When one changes things in the wrong manner, there is no wisdom. There will likely only be a schism. For example, one may want their significant other to begin to resume their normal activities and go about it the wrong way. A little encouragement can go a long way. Too hard of a push can create a price to pay.

4. What are you striving to change that you should not be trying to change regarding your loss and grief?

"Lord, grant me the wisdom to know what I am striving to change that I should not regarding my loss and grief?"

To be nosy can become very noisy. Trying to help in some cases may be in the best of intentions, but these efforts can result in futile dissensions. For example, one may want to change the way their partner is grieving. Each person needs the freedom to grieve in their own way. If a crisis occurs and a person begins to become stuck in their grief and becomes majorly depressed, then the family may need to intervene.

But initially, normal grief often cannot be distinguished from major depression. It is not so much about how long it takes a person to grieve. It becomes significant to realize if through the ups and downs of grief, one is gradually healing and reordering one's life.

5. What are some things that you do not know whether they are changeable or not changeable regarding your loss and grief?

"Lord, grant me the wisdom to distinguish between what can and cannot be changed regarding my loss and grief."

There are times when the decision is not clear

Whether something can be changed that is so dear.

This takes a time of prayer granting one an opportunity to
    explore
To help make the decision that one will not deplore.

For example, it may not yet be clear as to how to respond to the
situation surrounding the death. One needs to let the dust settle
before making a decision.

6. How can serenity, wisdom, and courage help me regarding my issues with loss and grief?

"Lord, help me to fully utilize the powerful traits of serenity, wisdom,
and courage to help me regarding my issues with loss and grief."

*The Serenity Prayer gives us meaning and purpose
And helps us to live life filled with a surplus.*

Imagine what you would look, feel, and act like if you were filled with
wisdom in dealing with grief.

Envision what you would look, feel, and act like if you were filled with
courage in dealing with grief.

Visualize what you would look, feel, and act like if you were filled with
serenity in dealing with grief.

In each state, how would your body language look?

What would be your facial expression?

How would you look out of your eyes?

What would the tone of your voice sound like?

What more would you be accomplishing?

How would you project your life to be different today, in one week, in one
month, in one year, in five years . . . ? Your life would be different indeed.

Cultivate these feelings. Develop a vision, and it will turn into a mission—a mission statement that is empowered. You can apply a vision and a mission to the vast array of your present and future challenges. Having a vision leads to a more specific mission. The Serenity Prayer can serve as fission to spark the energy to carry out the plan.

7. What do I need to change behaviorally regarding my loss and grief?

"Lord, grant me the wisdom to know what I need to change behaviorally regarding my loss and grief."

You need to affirm what you are doing well. Owning these strengths can help you feel swell. One can then take the next step with inspiration. Then the next step of growth will not be out of desperation. One can begin to row with the flow and experience life's progressive journey with a glow. For example, one may give themselves permission to cry or to be happy. Survivors' guilt can sometimes hinder reentering gradually the land of the living.

8. What do I need to change regarding my feelings and attitudes toward my loss and grief?

"Lord, grant me the wisdom to know what I need to change regarding my feelings and attitudes toward my loss and grief."

One's attitude is one's life's outlook. If it is negative, it can lead to a donnybrook. If it is positive, it can provide one a life's stance to celebrate each day with the attitude of wanting to dance. For example, one may change their attitude to give oneself time to grieve.

Chapter 7

Healing Trauma with Courage

A traumatic experience can knock you down.
You may feel that you cannot get up off the ground.

The Serenity Prayer raises these issues regarding trauma. One needs to know what to strive to change, how to change what one should change, what not to attempt to change, and what one cannot change. Growing in understanding and accomplishing these tasks in healing and coping with trauma certainly takes serenity, wisdom, and courage.

Engaging the Serenity Prayer with the issue of trauma can become a profitable soul-searching pilgrimage. The questions at the end of the chapter can help one ponder and apply the issues that this chapter raises in one's personal situation. In the process, you will be honing skills that will enable you to apply the prayer to all aspects of your life.

From Stress to Trauma to Recovery

> *Traumatic stress is the most challenging disturbance of all.*
> *It takes a community's understanding to help the person not to fall.*
> *The harrowing experience can overwhelm the mind, body, and spirit.*
> *One is left with symptoms that people may say are without merit.*
>
> *Serenity, courage, and wisdom can be used in their plight*
> *To begin the journey toward peace, which will help one feel all is right.*

This chapter will begin with stress and then move up the continuum to trauma. Concerning stress, we might say, "We can't live with it, and we can't live without it." The stress of a writing deadline motivates me to sit down at my computer and write. If we had no stress, we would be more than apathetic. Our lives would be pathetic. Stress is not all bad. It is part and parcel of living.

When our minds start racing and break the speed limit, we may have difficulty handling the curves that the highway of life brings. We need at times to check our mind's speedometer and see if we are cruising or speeding. The faster our mind speeds, the more life becomes a blur. We may miss some important road signs, keeping our lives in a stir. It is vital that we develop skills concerning slowing our minds down. If we do not, we may wear a continuous frown.

Deep breathing is a universal way of relaxing. Sports figures utilize this method to be able to handle the pressure of the suspenseful game. When a basketball player gets ready to shoot a free throw, you will see him/her virtually all the time take a deep breath before the shot. We can tend to do the reverse during pressure. When we experience stress and anxiety, we may have a tendency to breathe shallowly. Then, we receive less oxygen, and our anxiety will increase even more.

Shallow breathing can become a habit. One way to force one's self to breathe properly is to sit in a chair and bend over and breathe. This position forces one to breathe from one's diaphragm. By placing one's hands under one's stomach, one can feel the difference in how they breathe. The stomach does not expand when one shallowly breathes. When one does this exercise few times and then straightens up and speaks, one will likely notice that one's voice deepens. One will then be speaking more from one's diaphragm. One will also likely be more relaxed.

Monks have used meditation to clear the mind for centuries. Meditation involves closing one's eyes and letting one's mind gradually come to a resting place. It is like, in a spiritual sense, one is resting in the spirit. It is surrendering and sinking into the source of God's love. Love casts out fear.

Fear speeds up the mind. Of course, if a tiger runs after you, it is okay to get adrenalin rush to rush away from the tiger. Often, you may rush when you should hush. Rushing produces an internal fussing, which creates static in the radio of your lives. Having come to a resting place deeply within yourself is rejuvenating. With the mind, body, and spirit serene and quiet, you will have the reserve of alertness and energy to handle the curveballs that life may bring your way.

Recently, I was traveling through the desert at night. I did not realize how long it would be before I came to a place where I could fill up my tank. I was frightened that I may run out of gas. When I saw an exit sign signifying available gas, my mind, soul, and body came to a resting place. I was revived and at peace as my car received a full tank of gas. Deep breathing, meditation, and exercising and other methods can help you to have a full tank of gas. Your minds, bodies, and spirits can then be at rest.

When you left the womb and entered the world, you felt a jolt. The crying and the tears seemed like a revolt. The shocking change may have felt like a lightning bolt. You were comfortable, fed, and warm. In comparison, the world may have felt like a thunderstorm.

Stress increased as your responsibilities in the world increased. You had to breathe and drink. You felt some discomfort that life brings, but there is no growth without stress. Experiencing stress while moving out of your comfort zone can be reframed as growing pains. This stress can be positive if it is not overwhelming.

It now is a well-known fact that if one takes a baby bird out of the egg without the bird pecking its way out, it will not have the energy to develop. You need to stretch your physical, mental, emotional, and spiritual strength to grow in this world. You need to extend the envelope in order for you to write an ample letter of life. Moving out of your comfort zone is the catalyst for growth. Without this risk, you would never experience the adventure of learning a new skill or experiencing a new adventure.

Stress then can be your best friend. Stress can catapult you toward an adventurous life. The proper amount of stress can help you to operate at the peak of your potential. Embracing stress as a necessary part of life is important for living. Stress in life cannot be changed, but you can change how you handle stress.

It certainly helps to reduce stress in some instances. Too much stress can become distress. Some hospitals now take the baby directly from the womb to a warm water to lessen the jolt. Then they will take the infant up for air and cut the umbilical cord. The transition from the womb to the world is not such a jolt. It reduces distress for more optimal living. When you are under too much stress, your functioning on all levels is reduced. All of us at times will have more on our plate than we need at one time, and we can get emotional indigestion.

From one to ten, a stress level of five helps you to operate at the peak of your potential. A stress level of two would result in a lack of motivation. You may be apathetic. A stress level of seven or eight would begin to make the circumstances overwhelming, and your functioning would begin to deteriorate.

When I was taking ROTC in college, which is military training, we had a competitive playday. We were divided into teams. The challenge before us was to rotate ten times around the top of a Coke bottle with our head on top. Then we were to run to a Coke bottle some 150 feet away. Again, we were to rotate ten times and then run back to the first Coke bottle.

When it became my turn, I put my head on top of the first bottle and rotated ten times. I was so dizzy I wobbled like an inebriated person to the next Coke bottle. I felt an overwhelming challenge as I placed my extremely dizzy head on top of the Coke bottle. I was not looking forward to the shape I would in after the ten rotations. After the ten rotations, I was so dizzy I fell to the ground.

It was all I could do to get up and steady myself to slowly ramble to the first Coke bottle. My functioning increasingly deteriorated under the stress of the circular motion. I was in a severe state of disequilibrium. I was at the opposite state of the continuum of feeling centered.

Accepting what cannot be changed helps, but the stress that you absorb when you experience a trauma is in a different stressful category. Understanding the magnitude of stress resulting from trauma can help you to have more compassion to yourself and to others who have experienced such an overwhelming calamity. When trauma wrecks and rocks your soul, you need prayerful support to keep whole. Also, you need courage to be bold. Trauma overwhelms one's ability to cope. Of course, what I experienced was not traumatic. It is an analogy of what happens when an experience escalates into a real trauma. The event that I experienced can be looked back upon as a laughing matter. Real trauma is a huge matter. Taking trauma seriously truly matters.

All of us to some degree experience traumatic reactions. They may be on the lower end of the continuum. As the traumatic circumstances increase in stress, the greater they grip and rip our soul. The memories and feelings may stick with us. We need spiritual and human support to move toward becoming whole.

Nine-eleven (9/11) still rings in our ears as it echoes from the past. The reverberations from the earthquake still produce aftershocks and tremors. We are learning as a nation how to deal with trauma, which individuals have been dealing with since time began. Learning how to continue with our lives in a world out of control can be difficult. It is our challenge as individuals and as a nation to learn what we can change regarding terrorism and, in reality, what we cannot change.

Vietnam and 9/11 have brought traumatic dynamics to the fore. People understand better how extreme stress can hurt to the core. The symptoms are not easily resolved. It takes resolve to help the problems to begin to be solved. Coping and living on a level playing field with the most hideous of difficult people is stretching us as a nation and as a world to its limits. In a real sense, it is like the soul of America has been raped by the intrusion of the terrorist perpetrators. They have violated our country.

There are many hospitals that have a trauma center in which many specialists converge to help a person to recover as far as possible from the physical trauma. The care that they receive is beyond what is normal. We now know that a traumatic event can demand specialists to converge to help the person heal from the horrific emotional wound.

Many counselors and psychologists converged in New York to help people deal with the emotional trauma of the terrorist attack. Many people who escaped had near-death experiences. Some experienced the shock of losing loved ones or the shock of a near-death of a loved one. Some saw firsthand gruesome sights of people jumping from buildings. Some experienced smells that linger in their nostrils.

These experiences are deeply etched in the psychological and spiritual makeup of the people. Debriefing and other kinds of help were offered to help them begin to work through these feelings. The purpose concerned preventing them from developing deeper symptoms of the posttraumatic stress disorder (PTSD).

The firefighters and the policemen worked around the clock to strive to find survivors. Many of them experienced a toll on their emotional/spiritual well-being. They needed help from trauma specialists then and may still need periodic counseling. They needed to be debriefed and to begin to work through their feelings.

In relationship to psychological trauma, debriefing has become a method of helping people to talk through the difficulties of the trauma to help alleviate future symptoms. Debriefings help reduce lingering thoughts and feelings to help traumatized people gradually get the event behind them.

When one experiences a trauma, one is never exactly the same again. Collectively, 9/11 is possibly the greatest traumatic trauma that America has ever experienced on its own soil. Individuals have experienced similar levels of trauma in wars, robberies, abuse, etc., for aeons.

It is common to have some static remaining from the past. Perhaps some of this static is a good motivation to become more cautious. Some static is just a nuisance. When one has been hit blindsided once, one may wonder when it could reoccur. When Hugo hit Charleston, a few days later I was back on my porch putting the furniture back in placed. I thought, "It may come again!" The porch no longer felt like a safe haven.

It is a reality that America still waits with a feeling of what is coming next. This uncertainty makes it more of a challenge to come to terms with what happened on 9/11. We can get things behind us so they do not stare us in the face as often. But to most Americans, to some degree, feelings come back regarding 9/11. When one has been hit blindsided once, one may feel, "When is an attack going to happen again?"

As a whole, as a country we can at least temporarily become preoccupied with the deer-in-the-headlight look from this and other shocking traumatic experiences. We now have the possibility of terrorists getting the atomic bomb some time in the future, which magnifies 9/11 to unfathomable portions. We need to do what we can to change this threat, but we must live as a nation with what we cannot change or have not changed.

We need to keep some measure of serenity in the midst of uncertainty and unanswered questions. It is a truism that on any level, life remains a challenge. Life never becomes neat and tidy in its most peaceful times. There is always something that comes up to ripple the waters. We may have moments when events leave us in a daze. The surfacing complex set of traumatic feelings may feel like a maze.

Since trauma is the deepest level of stress, the Serenity Prayer is especially imperative. "Lord, help me to accept the things I cannot change, change the things I can, and the wisdom to know the difference." This attitude can keep the terrorist attack or any other trauma from continually terrorizing and paralyzing our souls. This is stress management at a high level.

Some people experiencing PTSD say, "My mind won't stop racing." They may have their emotional siren on all the time. Hypervigilant startled responses may be easily evoked. In some people, irritability or outburst may be experienced. As a logical result, concentration may be affected. People who have experienced a trauma also say, "The memory is worse than the event itself." Because of the traumatic, stressful event, the person may distort communication that is not meant. The statement may trigger incidents of the past, which may leave the person aghast.

Understanding the impact of emotional trauma is important in its recovery. It sets a foundation to deal with overwhelming events. The journey toward healing can begin. It has been only in recent times that we have taken a serious look at understanding emotional trauma. The Vietnam War pushed us to face the horrific symptoms of the posttraumatic stress disorder.

When one is traumatized, one does not need to have one's feelings shamed or discounted. It is important to be able to express them. People experience normal feelings from an abnormal, traumatic experience. Flashbacks may occur for some time. One will feel needless shame if one does not understand that recovery from such an experience is a journey.

It is a gradual experience of healing that enables a person to come to terms with a traumatic experience what one cannot change. As a person experiences traumatic symptoms of fight, freeze, or flight, their inner reactions and resulting behavior needs some light. Understanding and compassion can reduce their confusion and fright. After having experienced trauma, serenity is very challenging to find. It is not easy to recover one's peace of mind.

We need to have patience and understanding of others who have had the misfortune of experiencing a traumatic event. Also, we need to have patience with ourselves if a traumatic event has befallen us. The event can come up from time to time and stare us in the face. Flashbacks can be triggered as we experience reliving the shocking scenario.

I have conducted debriefings to help groups who have experienced a traumatic event. Debriefings are used to help begin to work through their feelings to prevent them from festering and moving toward a PTST diagnosis. *These are stories that represent what a debriefing is like. They are not accurately factual, but the characteristics of a debriefing process that is briefly shared are accurate.*

A youth group went white-water rafting in Tennessee. A freak accident occurred. One of the teenage boys was thrown off the boat, hit his head on a rock, and soon died. This tragedy naturally greatly affected the teenagers and adults who observed the event.

The group felt a sense of helplessness, which is universal in experiencing a traumatic event. They were left with questions and attempted spiritual answers regarding the calamity. It was a group of thirty in the debriefing session, which lasted approximately ninety minutes. There is a certain process in debriefing that helps people begin to work through feelings and thoughts that linger with them.

After the beginning of the meeting, a well-meaning man volunteered to read something beautiful that the teenager had recently written. I thanked him for his offer and told him that that letter would be especially meaningful toward the end of the session. It was premature to present something inspirational. He was striving to provide a positive atmosphere to allay the painful, puzzling feelings people were experiencing inside.

At the outset, attendees were asked a set of questions to give them an opportunity to tell the story regarding what they saw and experienced. Next, the questions began to become deeper regarding how this event was affecting the members now. Then, they began to bring up scenes, feelings, and thoughts that were sticking with them.

As some attendees shared, others began to experience sufficient trust to participate. They felt permission to verbalize the naturally negative feelings of hurt, anger, guilt, shock, and confusion. After the attendees had time to process the impact of the tragedy, I asked the man to read the letter that he had talked with me prior to the debriefing. As he read the inspirational letter written by the teenager, he was able to share some genuine tears. If he had read it at the beginning, he may have used the letter to keep himself and the group from sharing the natural emotions and thoughts resulting from experiencing a traumatic event.

Next is a second illustration that is also not factual. It does accurately explain debriefing and trauma. These were teenagers around thirteen years old. The event occurred in North Carolina. At the outset, some youth members were giving inappropriate responses. It was an effort to avoid dealing with how this event had impacted their lives. There was one particular youth that was trying to get the session off track. I went up to him and looked him in the eye, bending down to get at his same level, and said with a low voice. Your responses are inappropriate. Then the whole tenor of the group changed. They began to share dreams of the event. Feelings of grief of missing the injured youth leader were expressed. They shared in many ways the scene of the crime that lingered with them and the loss and grief that they felt.

The teenager who was initially striving to get the group off target thanked me for taking time to drive forty-five miles to lead the session. The healing process for the group had begun. They had the courage to open up and deal with normal feelings that result from an abnormal event.

The issues of control became more of a challenge in light of the effects of trauma. As a result of experiencing no control, one can feel unsafe in the world. A level of anxiety can become chronic. What is already on the plates of one's life seems to enlarge. This makes it even more important to understand the importance of self-care. The coping mechanisms that one has used in the past can be used in the present. Those can be enhanced, and new coping mechanisms can be added to the repertoire.

The twentieth century was called the *age of anxiety*. Our time in the twenty-first is on the way of being called the *age of terror*. One who has experienced trauma has experienced terror. This shocking experience can create a chronic sense of uneasiness that can periodically surface as terror. Serenity is nowhere to be found.

A repertoire of resources along with the Serenity Prayer combined together can gradually bring serenity. A good nutritional diet becomes even more important during times of traumatic stress. Caffeine, particularly for some people, can become fiendish during stressful times. One can feel a temporary lift through this drug. When a crisis erupts, caffeine in the system only multiplies the traumatic effects, rendering one with less coping ability.

Normal stressors can become magnified, and the terror alert can be increased without any substantial reason. Adrenaline pours through the body's system during a crisis. We do not need adrenaline in our system when there is a stress level that does not reach the level of terror. The adrenaline rush may cause us to be rushing around like a chicken with its head cut off.

It is now commonly known that B vitamins help in dealing with stress. Exercise is another way to combat the inner stress that we feel. One does not have to be an athlete to gain benefits from exercise. Simply walking thirty minutes a day can have a great effect on the way we experience stress during the day.

In any exercise program, it is important that one starts small and gradually build up. "No pain, no gain" can be taken to the extreme. Also, it is wise to contact your physician before beginning an exercise program or taking any vitamins.

Monks for hundreds of years have used a prayer similar to "God, have mercy on me." This has been a prayer of meditation to pray over and over again until mercy, love, and peace overflows from one's soul. There are other prayers that can help. "God, come into my mind, my body, my spirit, and my feelings. Love me and make me whole." When we are frazzled to the max, we need the comforting presence of God. When life takes the rugs out from under us, we need a multitude of hugs. Sometimes one may need to see a therapist and possibly a doctor to help in coping with the aftereffects of a trauma.

Wisdom

It takes wisdom to begin the recovery from a trauma. A traumatized person has been through an indescribable drama. Wisdom says that they need to reach out for help. The person needs someone to understand how the experience felt.

Courage

To have the courage to face the traumatic experience is of such heroic proportions that the person needs deference to slowly reenter the land of the living. One needs community support to keep their courage continuing. Reaching out helps the person to be on a journey of recovery. Slowly one will be experiencing a true life-giving discovery.

Serenity

One needs growing amounts of serenity to heal one's soul. Serenity helps the deep, anguishing pain to lessen its toll. Serenity is experienced in brief moments at first. They can linger longer as one quenches some of their unquenchable thirst.

The following guiding questions are adapted to the chapter on trauma. These thought-provoking questions are to help you ponder personal applications of the Serenity Prayer. The resulting soul-searching exercise can aid you to more fully experience the Serenity Prayer lifestyle as you apply this prayer to all aspects of your daily life.

These questions embodied in the Serenity Prayer then can begin a personal lifelong quest in becoming more skillful in living the Serenity Prayer lifestyle. Then the Serenity Prayer can become increasingly embedded in your life. The prayer can help smooth out the edges of life and prevent your lifestyle from becoming coarse. The voice of your life will not become hoarse. The Serenity Prayer then is a great spiritual resource to help you keep the course.

Coaching Questions: Helping You Heal from a Traumatizing Event

Remember:

You are not starting from scratch. You have long since been hatched. Your efforts have not gone for naught. You can be commended for what you have already wrought.

These questions and thoughts are for the purpose of serving as a personal coaching friend. They can give you the opportunity to prayerfully brainstorm to surface the challenges and solutions in your particular situation. You may find an opportunity to build upon what you are already doing well and take another step forward.

Engaging the Serenity Prayer with the issue of trauma can become a profitable soul-searching pilgrimage. In the process, you will be honing skills that will enable you to apply the prayer to all aspects of your life.

1. **What do you need to accept that you cannot change regarding your issue with trauma?**

"Lord, grant me the wisdom to know what I need to accept and that I cannot change regarding my issues with trauma."

It is very difficult to let go of the unalterable aspects of life. They can bring us to the altar when we falter in reducing our internal strife.

2. **What do you need to change that you can change regarding your issues with trauma?**

"Lord, grant me the wisdom to know what I should change regarding my issues with trauma."

We can make a difference that counts, and the worthless behaviors we will renounce.

For example, one can learn from their past mistakes.

3. What are some things you can change that you may be striving to change in the wrong manner with regard to your trauma?

"Lord, help me to realize what I have been changing in the wrong manner regarding my issues with trauma."

Does the end justify the means?

Is the process worthy of the progress?

Does the manner of change have good manners?

It can help by thinking of an example of what you have changed in a healthy way. Begin from a positive feeling.

4. What are you wrongly striving to change regarding your trauma?

"Lord, grant me the wisdom to know what I have been striving to change that I should not be trying to change regarding my issues with trauma."

5. What are some things that you do not know whether they are changeable or unchangeable regarding your issues with your trauma?

"Lord, grant me the wisdom to know what can be changed and what cannot be changed regarding my issues with trauma."

There are times when the decision is not clear whether something can be changed that is so dear. For example, one needs to take a time of prayer to explore to help make the decision that one will not deplore.

6. How can serenity, wisdom, and courage help you deal with your issues of your trauma?

"Lord, grant me the guidance to fully utilize the powerful, dynamic traits of serenity, wisdom, and courage to help me deal with my issues of trauma."

> *The Serenity Prayer gives us meaning and purpose*
> *And helps us to live life filled with an overflowing surplus.*

Imagine what you would look, feel, and act like if you were filled with wisdom regarding dealing with your issues with your trauma.

Envision what you would look, feel, and act like if you were filled with courage regarding your issues with your trauma.

Visualize what you would look, feel, and act like if you were filled with serenity regarding your issues with your trauma.

In each state, how would your body language appear?

What would be your facial expression?

How would you look out of your eyes?

What would the tone of your voice sound like?

What more would you be accomplishing?

Envision how others would respond to you differently.

How would you project your life to be different today, in one week, in one month, in one year, in five years . . . ? Your life would be different indeed.

Cultivate these feelings. Get a vision, and it will turn into a mission—a mission statement that is empowered. One can make a general mission statement. You can apply a vision and a mission to the vast array of your present and future challenges. The Serenity Prayer can serve as fission to spark the energy to carry out the plan.

7. **What do you need to change behaviorally regarding your issues with your trauma?**

"Lord, grant me the wisdom to know what I need to change behaviorally regarding my issues with shame."

> You need to affirm what you are doing well.
> Owning these strengths can help you feel swell.
>
> You can then take the next step with inspiration.
> Then the next step of growth will not be out of desperation.
>
> One can begin to go with the flow
> And experience life's progressive journey with a glow.
>
> For example, one may need to change behaviors that are symptoms
> of shame. Many addictions and impulsive behaviors can be ways
> of striving to deal with the pain of shame.

8. **What do you need to change regarding my feelings and attitudes concerning your issues with trauma?**

"Lord, grant me the wisdom to know what I need to change regarding my feelings and attitudes concerning my issues with my trauma."

> One's attitude is one's life's outlook.
> If it is negative it can lead to a donnybrook.
> If it is positive it can provide one a life's stance.
> To celebrate each day with the attitude of wanting to dance.

Chapter 8

Shortchanging Shame:
Taming the Shaming Malaise

Shame chews up one's self-esteem and spits it out.

The Serenity Prayer raises these issues regarding taming shame. One needs to know what to strive to change, how to change what one should change, what not to attempt to change, and what one cannot change. Taming shame and turning shame feelings into feelings of dignity certainly takes serenity, wisdom, and courage.

Engaging the Serenity Prayer with the issue of shame can become a profitable soul-searching pilgrimage. The questions at the end of the chapter can help you ponder and apply the issues that this chapter raises. In the process, you will be honing skills that will enable you to apply the prayer to all aspects of your life.

If we have a shame-based personality, we may have a particular challenge in getting to first base regarding gaining control of control matters. Shame can ripple throughout our lives and destroy our peace. Our control issues may be infected by the shame malaise. At the core of shame is a feeling of being out of control. Negative feelings can go deeper into feeling helpless, hopeless, and worthless.

False humiliation can result in an attitude that one cannot change themselves. One may feel that that have not made a mistake. One may feel that one is a mistake. Then, one may come to the conclusion that there are no redeeming virtues to build upon. The lights are out in the ball field. There is a power failure as one does not feel empowered.

Shame can result in one feeling lame. The feelings may be so demoralizing that it is hard to give them a name. Shame robs one of their sense of dignity. To feel humiliated is to feel hated and with foreboding enmity.

Guilt can be good in helping us to grow toward being better people. We can learn from our poor choices. Life can become a better experience. Contrarily, shame can put us on a downward slide, making life a bitter experience. Life can become a difficult pill to swallow. Many people struggle with shame. It can come from many sources.

Finding these sources is not a way of blaming someone else with our challenges with shame. It is a way to formulate a strategy to gain control of shame. Then we can move to having genuine fame in our own minds. We can gain a sense of recognition, which can result in a feeling of distinction. We can be lifted up to see our value for what it is. One may or may not be able to find the source of the shame. Treating the symptoms is important in both cases.

Shame can result from painful feelings that are just under the surface. When this pain is experienced, you may place shameful words of explanation as to why the pain is there. Derogatory remarks may be said as you feel that you deserve the pain. Shame then takes the air out of your sails as you may feel that you need to be continually punished. The guilt that you feel is false guilt. The false guilt is shame.

You may justify why you feel so dirty by saying that it must be because you are despicable. Shame is a formidable hindrance in accepting what you cannot change. Shame causes you to stew in your own juice. People with addictions are often shame-based. They may, to some degree, falsely interpret their painful surfacing feelings as meaning that they are rotten to the core.

Shame can come from abuse and trauma. This sense of disgrace preoccupies one with exaggerating one's limitations. This feeling of humiliation falsifies one's worth. It reduces the reality that we are priceless to the sick illusion that we are worthless. Shame can be like a toxin in the bloodstream, infecting the mind, the body, and the spirit.

When one realizes that the pain is coming from something that was unpreventable, the Serenity Prayer becomes of paramount importance. One aspect of healing is accepting what one cannot change. One may continue to live with some level of pain, but the shame can be tamed. Then pain can be more manageable. Pain then will have a different texture. You can gradually move toward healing as shame stops lashing the wounds.

The Serenity Prayer can wrap its arms around the pain. Then healing can take place. What you say to yourself about your pain can change your attitude. You are not responsible for the pain. You can put your energies into your real responsibility, which is how you deal with your pain.

Your efforts can go to providing a climate that can help heal your soul. Shame may linger, or it may briefly raise its ugly head periodically. When the humiliation of shame surfaces, you can gradually see it for what it is and put a period on your negative, shameful thoughts.

Many years ago when I was a chaplain intern at Baptist Medical Center, I saw a painting displayed in the hallway beyond the foyer that grabbed my attention. It was a painting of a forest that had been blackened by the blaze of a ferocious fire. Soot and embers were everywhere. I pondered what the painting could mean. Then I saw in the bottom-right corner a small, budding flower.

You can positively reframe how you interpret the experience that this painting depicts. It is natural to focus on the blackened forest and allow it to dominate and characterize one's life. One can reinterpret the traumatic experience that this painting depicts. The blackened forest does not define the person. The real person is the small, budding, red flower.

One can then realize that the forest was blackened by a ferocious fire of which it was not responsible. A person that has been abused has been burned and is not responsible for the resulting ravaging pain. One is responsible regarding how one handles the pain.

Efforts can be utilized to water the flower and let it grow until it moves from the background of one's life to the foreground. Then the person will feel the defining moment when the journey from shaming toward healing begins. The throbbing pain has a different texture. It is now not robbing one of one's life. The flower of the person's life is blossoming in the midst of the surrounding soot and ashes.

When I find myself triggered in the throes of shame, it helps me to pray the prayer, "Lord, forgive me for shaming myself." This prayer helps me to snap out of a noxious trance and come back to the present moment. I am no longer stuck. I can change what I can.

One can be moved from preoccupation to occupying and dwelling in the land of the living. Serenity can become one of the amenities of acceptance of yourself. This peace in your soul is a priceless trait. You are enabled to be comfortable in your own skin. The impact of shame is being shortchanged. You can move from feeling like damaged goods toward feeling like a good person.

Shame is not being comfortable in one's own skin. It is feeling hell from within. Shame can be demoralizing. One is stuck and not actualizing. When one tames shame, it loses its power. One is able to live with peace every hour. The symptoms of shame resulting from the inner pain are not as operative, and persons can focus on operating their own lives toward worthy, purposeful goals.

Serenity is peace with oneself, with one's circumstances, and with one's past, present, and future. In shame, the court has made its decision, and the person is found guilty when there is no guilt. The person has been given a life sentence of shame without parole. Serenity sentences a person to a peaceful life.

There is a company where one can order dead roses that can be sent as a gag gift to someone one does not like. Shame sends a gag gift that can gag the mind, heart, and soul. Then the gagged soul may live in quiet desperation or enraged activation. Shame makes one emotionally and spiritually homeless. One does not feel at home with themselves.

Much has been written about shame. It needs to be seen through the eyes of the Serenity Prayer to provide a transformation from shameful feelings of disgrace to a feeling of grace and unconditional love. Grace can lift the painful sense of false guilt to a sense of peaceful acceptance.

Shame is the opposite of serenity. Serenity gives one dignity. Shame brings indignity. Shame maims the soul and leaves it lying on the road wounded and dying. It continues to distort the value of the person by lying. Shame deprives one of purpose and meaning. It leaves the soul silently screaming. Shame makes one attuned to the people who are jeering. When the shame is gone, one can hear the people who are cheering. Shame puts a sign on our backs that says "kick me." Serenity can give us a kick out of living with glee.

The soul can experience becoming crippled by shame. This shame can handicap one and hold one hostage. Shame provides intrusive thoughts that can torture the soul. It is a ball and chain that weighs one down. The Serenity Prayer can gradually anchor one's soul. This precious spiritual resource can grant us a sense of stability, security, and a place of centeredness to get on with the business of living.

Shame blinds one to what one cannot and can change. Shame has no wisdom, courage, or serenity. As a result, shame has no redeeming virtue. It is like a tumor that is malignant that needs to be surgically removed. It contaminates the body as it spreads and affects all of one's life. It is false guilt working overtime and exhausting the soul.

Guilt is the natural feeling of wrongdoing. Shame in the body can feel like weeds that chokes the grass of a beautiful lawn. Forgiveness of guilt can choke out the weeds.

Forgiveness rights the wrong and sets one free to live a more peaceful and productive life. Guilt unattended may not only cause one to run from other people; it may also cause one to run from themselves. They do not want to face their guilt. They do not want to change what needs to be changed. One needs courage and wisdom to deal with guilt and change what one can to move toward serenity.

A vital part of this prayer is changing what we can change. It takes both wisdom to see what we can change and how we should change it and courage to be the catalyst to activate us to do what is necessary for the change-making progress.

> *Striving for excellence is free from shame.*
> *One can have the freedom to fail on the way to fame.*

Perfectionism can become a symptom of shame. With one mistake one can feel lost. One always feels like they come up short as one cannot get perfectionism to abort. Perfectionism inhibits one from changing what one can change for fear that the change will not be in their ability range. To give one's best effort is frightening at best. It may be terrifying, which may squelch their quest.

> *Perfectionism can become toxic and penetrate the soul.*
> *As a result one may feel very old.*

Perfectionism is a serious obstacle that can result in a damaging debacle. Perfectionism can catapult us into a state of inertia, fearing failing. It can also place us in a fit of frenzy to accomplish a task while railing. Perfectionism and shame go hand in hand. This devilish duo creates disturbed people all over this land. Serenity is infected by these rogues. Through the eyes of the Serenity Prayer, shame can be driven out in droves.

Perfectionism can be defeated by the Serenity Prayer. Accepting what cannot be changed will not be hard to bear. Courage will fight the shame within and help the person to risk and begin. The journey can be filled with mistakes as the shameless person plows ahead for high stakes. He will plant many seeds in the fertile rows, and his efforts will pay off as the fruits of his labor grow.

Perfectionism infects peaceful serenity. When one makes a mistake, it can feel like a gash in one's heart, and one cannot stop the bleeding. It makes it more difficult for one to get on with the future and learn from the mistake. It is important for us to take dead aim at our goals, but it does not have to be all or nothing. No one can change a past mistake. With perfectionism, the glitch itches, and scratching does no good. It only produces a gash.

> *A mistake can become a stepping-stone.*
> *Perfectionism hurts to the bone.*

Accepting what we cannot change can be the cure for perfectionism. Perfectionism disturbs the waters, and there is no peace. Many sports figures have made a mistake, and it cost the team a win. The coach may use the words "shake it off." The coach realizes that if one continues to think about the past mistake, they will not be able to get their minds on the next game.

If one golfer misses one shot, he will not hit the next shot well if he is still punishing himself for the mistake. Perfectionism can be a part of the shame-based personality. They are so ashamed of the past that they cannot be in the present.

> *With perfectionism one feels that they never reach the pinnacle,*
> *And it can leave one with the attitude of being very cynical.*

One deserves to let this prayer saturate the soul. "God, grant me the serenity to accept the things that I cannot change and then pick one's self up and get ready for the next game of life." Then the thoughts of the mistake will not hold one hostage. They have faded into the background and lost their grip. They may actually benefit one because one has learned from the malfunction.

Perfectionism then can be one's pitfall and can paralyze one's life as one is stuck in torment about the past mistake. It can be a small pimple that one focuses on incessantly. There is a point in which one takes oneself too seriously. This kind of seriousness is a detrimental mistake. Perfectionism then within itself is a mistake. One can never be perfect.

One can be like an ostrich putting one's head in the sand and not dealing with the challengers that are passing by. One is too busy punishing one's self to face the natural ups and downs of life. A mistake can cause one to search one's soul to learn. Perfectionism can parch one resulting in a soul burn. With grace and serenity, one will not be preoccupied by past failures. One will be occupied by the hope of future treasures.

Finally, one may act out their pain in varying degrees of destructive acts. One may also cover up their pain by drugs or alcohol to escape the pain, which leaves them at a loss instead of a gain. There is help when one recognizes their needs. Then the destructive acts toward oneself can turn into constructive deeds.

Wisdom

It takes wisdom to not let the feelings of shame reign. It can feel like it is engulfing a person who does not feel the same. Who am I in the midst of the helpless, hopeless, worthless feelings? Wisdom says I am not what the feelings say while I am reeling. Wisdom says I am a person experiencing deep pain from the past. It does not define me, and it will not last.

Courage

Courage states that I can stare the pain down. I can do something about my shame's continuous frown. I can tell it is not going to take charge of me. I am going to tell you to go, and I will be free. As it surfaces I may still feel the underlying pain, but it will be less without the *burden of shame*.

Serenity

Serenity is to find the real me separate from the pain. When one knows the pain does not define them, it is a peaceful gain. Serenity stares pain in the face and states that you are not welcomed in this place. The person can be lifted from their triggered trance, which surfaced feelings originating long ago that need to be lanced. You can know that you are not defined by what you are feeling and thinking. You are not what the thoughts resulting from the feelings are telling you are. You may say to the false thoughts, "I am not what you say I am. Scram. You are a pain surfacing from a deep, emotional wound from the distant past that comes to the surface from time to time. You will not ring my chime. I may feel your hurt, but I will not response by discounting my worth."

The following guiding questions are adapted to the chapter on shame. These thought-provoking questions are to help you ponder personal applications and implications of the Serenity Prayer. The resulting soul-searching exercise can aid you to more fully experience the Serenity Prayer lifestyle as you apply this prayer to all aspects of your daily life.

These questions embodied in the Serenity Prayer then can begin a personal, lifelong quest in becoming more skillful in living the Serenity Prayer lifestyle. Then the Serenity Prayer can become increasingly embedded in your life. The prayer can help smooth out the edges of life and prevent your lifestyle from becoming coarse. The voice of your life will not become hoarse. The Serenity Prayer then is a great spiritual resource to help you keep the course.

Remember:

You are not starting from scratch. You have long since been hatched. In your life, your efforts have not gone for naught. You can be commended for what you have already wrought.

These questions and thoughts are for the purpose of serving as a personal friend. They can give you the opportunity to prayerfully brainstorm to surface the challenges and solutions in your particular situation. You may find an opportunity to build upon what you are already doing well and take another step forward. Engaging the Serenity Prayer with the issue of shame can become a profitable, soul-searching pilgrimage.

Coaching Questions: Helping You Tame Your Shame

1. What do you need to change that you can change regarding your issues with shame?

"Lord, grant me the wisdom to know what I should change regarding my issues with shame."

We can make a difference that counts, and the worthless behaviors, we will renounce.

For example, one can learn from their past mistakes.

2. What are some things you can change that you may be striving to change in the wrong manner with regard to your shame?

"Lord, help me to realize what I have been changing in the wrong manner regarding my issues with shame."

Does the end justify the means?

Is the process worthy of the progress?

Does the manner of change have good manners?

It can help by thinking of an example of what you have changed
in a healthy way. Begin from a positive feeling.

When one changes things in the wrong way, there is no serenity.
There will likely only be enmity. When one changes things in the wrong
manner, there is no wisdom. There will likely only be a schism.

For example, trying to eradicate shame with perfectionism will not work.
One may be too critical of oneself and too critical of another's quirk.

3. What are you wrongly striving to change regarding shame?

"Lord, grant me the wisdom to know what I have been striving to change
that I should not be trying to change regarding my issues with shame."

Trying to make improvements may be in the best of intentions, But
these efforts can result in futile dissensions. For example, one may try to
eradicate shame by striving to be perfect or by overreacting and blaming
someone else for their own mistakes.

4. What are some things that you do not know whether they are changeable or unchangeable regarding your issues with shame?

"Lord, grant me the wisdom to know what can be changed and what
cannot be changed regarding my issues with shame."

There are times when the decision is not clear whether something can be
changed that is so dear. For example, one needs to take a time of prayer to
explore to help make the decision that one will not deplore. Sometimes one
may not be able to find out where the shame originated. It can be difficult
to know whether one can gain that insight or just let it go.

5. How can serenity, wisdom, and courage help you deal with your issues of shame?

"Lord, grant me the guidance to fully utilize the powerful, dynamic traits of serenity, wisdom, and courage to help me deal with my issues of shame."

The Serenity Prayer gives us meaning and purpose
And helps us to live life filled with an overflowing surplus.

Imagine what you would look, feel, and act like it you were filled with wisdom regarding dealing with your issues with shame.

Envision what you would look, feel, and act like if you were filled with courage regarding your issues with shame.

Visualize what you would look, feel, and act like if you were filled with serenity regarding your issues with shame.

In each state, how would your body language appear?

What would be your facial expression?

How would you look out of your eyes?

What would the tone of your voice sound like?
What more would you be accomplishing?

Envision how others would respond to you differently.

How would you project your life to be different today, in one week, in one month, in one year, in five years . . . ? Your life would be different indeed.

Cultivate these feelings. Get a vision, and it will turn into a mission—a mission statement that is empowered. One can make a general mission statement. You can apply a vision and a mission to the vast array of your present and future challenges. The Serenity Prayer can serve as fission to spark the energy to carry out the plan.

6. What do you need to change behaviorally regarding your issues with shame?

"Lord, grant me the wisdom to know what I need to change behaviorally regarding my issues with shame."

> You need to affirm what you are doing well.
> Owning these strengths can help you feel swell.
> You can then take the next step with inspiration.
> Then the next step of growth will not be out of desperation.
> One can begin to go with the flow.
> And experience life's progressive journey with a glow.

> For example, one may need to change behaviors that are symptoms of shame. Many addictions and impulsive behaviors can be ways of striving to deal with the pain of shame.

7. What do I need to change regarding my feelings and attitudes concerning my issues with shame?

"Lord, grant me the wisdom to know what I need to change regarding my feelings and attitudes concerning my issues with shame."

> One's attitude is one's life's outlook.
> If it is negative it can lead to a donnybrook.
> If it is positive it can provide one a life's stance.
> To celebrate each day with wanting to dance.

> For example, one makes a mistake. One is not a mistake. A donnybrook is a complex set of problems that is a great threat to one's well-being and serenity.

Part 4

The Serenity Prayer:
A Coach for Healthy Relationships

Chapter 9

Good Boundaries:
Bound for the Promised Land

Healthy boundaries keep one in the game of life.
Knowing who to let in and how close can prevent much strife.

The Serenity Prayer raises these issues regarding boundaries. You need to know what to strive to change, how to change what you should change, what not to attempt to change, and what you cannot change. Growing in understanding and accomplishing these tasks in setting healthy boundaries certainly takes serenity, wisdom, and courage.

Engaging the Serenity Prayer with the issue of boundaries can become a profitable soul-searching pilgrimage. In relationships there needs to be enough space to prevent a wreck. Relationships can ultimately collide if there is too little distance in their togetherness. Also, a relationship can become derailed if there is too much distance for true intimacy. The partners need to bond and feel very near to each other. If they are too close without ample distance, they may become a bother. The Serenity Prayer can provide a mentoring coach to help boundaries to be found to free one from feeling bound.

In terms of relational control, boundaries give balance. "Lord, help us change what we can." To implement that prayerful request in a constructive manner, you need to understand boundaries. If we are people who are over controlling, we become intrusive and unwelcomed guests in other people's space in an attempt to change them. Then boundaries will become out of balance. The fate of the relationship can be held in a balance.

If you have allowed someone to violate your space, you may feel that they are being held hostage and have no breathing room. You may freeze and set yourself up to become a victim. The deer-in-the-headlight look does not fare well. You may not get out of the way of oncoming traffic. As a result, you may become injured by the person who has intruded upon your space. Consequently, if you indiscriminately let others in your space and do not get out of their way, you may feel like your life is a wreck. As you balance your life, you need space. Boundaries give you your needed private place.

Knowing what to change and how to change what you can change can prevent you from sticking your noses in the wrong places. For example, intruding upon the responsibilities of others and taking them on as your own can overwhelm your mind, body, and spirit. You may begin to slowly sink in the quicksand and become the victim. When you do not know where you should be sticking your noses, you may feel the prick of thorns instead of the smell of roses.

The spouse often enables the behavior of the person with an alcohol problem. For example, they may strive to cushion the blow of the repercussions of their spouse's drinking. The spouse rescues the problem drinker from the consequences of their behavior, enabling their destructive behavior to continue. This enabling behavior inhibits their spouse's impetus to reach out for help.

The enabler becomes a chronic safety net. This net prevents the person with alcoholism from having the opportunity of hitting bottom and bouncing back up into a new way of life. The pattern of sticking one's nose in the business of the person with an alcohol problem can indeed erode the sanity of the enabler. Their needs are getting lost. An enabler can increase their fervor, placing their lives on a feverously unhealthy path. Well-meaning, overzealous fervor can backfire on the server.

Changing this pattern can be a win-win for both the person with alcoholism and the spouse. The person with alcoholism can find their true selves and begin a path of growth. The spouse can be freed from the entanglement of enabling behavior.

There is also the danger that the person with the alcohol problem will not, at least at this time, change. They now will know that the ball is in their court. If they do not change, they may have to go to court. They will begin to have to look at themselves in the mirror. The consequences of their behavior may bring a sense of horror.

The spouse will learn when the ball is in their court and when the ball is in their spouse's court. As a result, boundaries can be like floodgates keeping the unrealistic demands and expectations of others from flooding their lives. Boundaries can give us a healthy sense of control to keep conniving people's behavior from taking its toll.

Just as the ocean waves coming ashore can erode the beauty of the beach, lacking boundaries can cause erosion in our emotional and spiritual health. Millions of dollars are spent each year to help the beaches recover from the devastating impact of erosion. Billions of dollars are spent helping people recover from stress-related illnesses resulting from weak boundaries. These illnesses result from not taking care of themselves and letting the wolf "huff and puff and blow the house down."

Boundaries are preventative tools. They are crucial in creating a buffer to protect us from others who may infringe upon our lives. This buffer can prevent us from being buffeted by insensitive, intrusive behavior. We need to draw a line in the sand to prevent us from succumbing to a person's unreasonable demand.

When a fly or mosquito violates our boundaries, we become agitated and do all we can to eradicate the intruder. An insect repellent keeps them at bay. Then we can relax at the bay.

A healthy sense of self-esteem can be the foundation of building a boundary to keep others from violating our boundaries. We are in control. This foundation can prevent us from floundering. We are the executives of our lives. The decisions that we make can allow a balance between saying yes and saying no. We can prevent ourselves from being fodder eaten up by the hungry, ravenous, selfish appetites of others.

On the other hand, we can also declare a healthy yes, which can enable us to be productive at our very best. The promiseland can be within our grasp as we use healthy, balanced boundaries to enable us to complete our task.

Unhealthy Boundaries: Who Is Most Susceptible?

When boundaries have been broken when one was a child, one's behavior can violate others as one becomes wild. An opposite reaction is not using boundaries as protection. The person may open their door at the slightest suggestion.

The people who have severe problems with boundaries often have been struck with repeated blows emotionally and/or physically. Their boundaries may have been violated with verbal, physical, or sexual abuse. They may be left broken emotionally. Boundaries can prevent one from being misused. Boundaries can ward off being abused. With boundaries, one can gradually heal until the damage is diminished. Then one's healing will be almost finished.

Having no boundaries may strike a chord within us to be free. It is exciting to see films of horses in the Wild West running free.

We are not created to run wild. On the other hand, we do not need to be corralled like wild horses and put in a fence with a locked gate. Otherwise, we will say "nay nay nay" like the corralled horse. Boundaries need gates that will enable us to receive a helping hand. Then we can become empowered to change what we can.

Having a low self-esteem resulting from boundary violations may make it difficult to say no. Saying yes to please others without regard to one's own needs leaves one vulnerable. One may allow oneself to be used or manipulated. On the other hand, people with low self-esteem may try to feel better by acting out their pain by bullying others or violating others' needs. They look for vulnerable targets or people who act in their pain.

People with low self-worth may deprecate themselves and focus primarily on others. This is fulfilling to them as it helps them to avoid focusing on their own inner pain. It is often said that one way to feel better is to help someone else. This is certainly true to a point. By helping others to the extreme, a person can run out of steam, making their goal an impossible dream.

With care and persistence, one can recover from control malfunctions. One can, through the help of others, reconstruct their lifestyle and produce the beautiful person that God intended for them to become. They can find their broken inner child emerging from the hammer blows to become beautifully sculptured. They can fashion a life that becomes a fashion statement. In this fashion, one can say yes and no and recognize how to reason. This fashion statement can emphatically declare that they have a right to honor their limits and move toward their possible dreams.

Boundaries: A Balancing Act

Balancing yes and no prevents too much from being on one's plate. This balance prevents one from developing a chronic, emotional ache. Gaining a sense of healthy boundaries is truly a balancing act. I remember as a child, during recess, wanting to play on a seesaw. I found a friend much larger than myself and began to try to seesaw. It was very difficult if not impossible because the seesaw was weighted down on my friend's side. There was not a nice up-and-down flow. The weight distribution was not equal, and it became very tiring.

When one balances the seesaw, the experience can truly become a hee-haw. If the seesaw is imbalanced, it can become the last straw.

Life is a marathon, not a mad dash. We will not finish the race carrying someone continuously on our backs.

You cannot finish the race with someone on your back.
Becoming overly burdened by others can create an emotional crack.

Then you will not have the coping skills to healthily act.
An unbalanced life then can become a painful fact.

It needs to be noted that sometimes there are no easy answers. A person with a handicapped child has a particularly tough challenge in setting boundaries. The task can at times become overwhelming, and gaining proper help may not always be readily available.

It is different when we are dealing with a crisis or a trauma. This is a temporary situation that can try one's soul. One may have to overextend themselves for a period of time. These boundary issues pertain to a lifestyle of overextending ourselves. The seesaw in the flow of life is not balanced. Life is not working well and is not fulfilling.

Oftentimes, the oldest child chooses a lifestyle that becomes overly responsible. Many executives are the oldest child. Some of the strongest leaders are older children. But many burn out because they do not set boundaries. They will be working when they need to be soaking up love and having enriching experiences that feed their souls. One needs someone to help them to think, or their lives may go down the brink. Self-esteem means that one gives but also takes care of themselves. They do not always have to make gifts like Santa Claus' little elves.

Self-esteem is not arrogant. Healthy self-esteem helps one to balance life and not be sucked dry by life's demands. In a balanced seesaw experience, the push of one person gives the other person a nice ride. Then, the initial pusher receives a nice ride as the other person pushes down. These boundaries help life to flow more "gently down the stream," and we will not buckle under the heavy weight of another person. Self-esteem helps one's life not to become lost in the shuffle. One knows when their feathers are beginning to be ruffled.

Boundaries: Not the Same for Everyone

Regarding boundaries, there is no cookie-cutter production line for all to follow. We have individual differences. Healthy boundaries in one person may be different from that of another person. Healthy boundaries for each person can be unique. Some people need more space to function at their peak.

For example, a dog's boundaries are very different than a cat's. A dog will immediately respond when its master calls. A cat's behavior may communicate, "I will be in touch with you later." At times cats seem to be aloof to their own world. Dogs are more extroverted, and they need much more attention from their master.

They need less time for themselves than a cat, and each style works. If it is not broken, do not fix it. In comparison to someone else, your boundaries may seem unhealthy. Appearances may be deceiving as you have a different mental and emotional makeup.

Consequently, just as cats and dogs have differences in boundaries, humans have differences as well. The range of healthy differences may not be as wide as dogs and cats, but extroverts are going to be more like dogs.

They need less boundaries for alone time. Introverts are like cats in that they can be contented spending more time by themselves.

Thus, extroverts often marry introverts. They seem to complement each other. One can be the center of attention, and the other can feel comfortable being in the background. The extrovert can be a good talker, and the introvert can be a good listener. The extrovert may be intense, and the introvert may be calm. These complementary traits can have a calming effect for the extrovert and can energize the introvert.

However, these qualities that initially attracted the couple can later begin to create conflict. The extrovert may wonder why the introvert wants to leave the party so early. They may fight like cats and dogs. Couples then must be sensitive to each other's differences so they will be able to handle conflicts less reactively. Each person has different needs in being alone. These needs must be honored, or conflict can cut to the bone. One partner, to gain distance, may push their partner away. That is the only way they feel they can keep them at bay.

Maybe that is why dogs generally do not like cats. The boundaries are at two ends of the spectrum. On the other hand, couples can like each other. They can compromise and enjoy the complementary aspects of their personalities. *The relationship can be viable as both vie for a successful connection.*

Boundaries: They Give Us our Identity

Healthy boundaries define who we are.
We say yes and no to keep ourselves from becoming ajar.
Unhealthy boundaries may become a jarring experience.

As we look at a map of the United States, each state is easily distinguishable by boundaries. Each state has a unique shape. As people, we gain our identity by the boundaries that we set. We know where we end and other people begin. Two questions are raised in our identity. "Who am I, and who am I not?" Boundaries tell us what state the body of land is and what territory is not a part of the state.

I was born as an identical twin. My brother and I dressed alike, and many people called us twins. They could not tell us apart. It was cute for us to be together, but it hindered gaining a sense of identity. Gradually, we emerged as two separate people with unique strengths and weaknesses.

If boundaries were too rigid, people would not be able to travel around the United States and learn the uniqueness of each state. In the same light, when people have rigid boundaries, people then will not get to know them. Boundaries need to be permeable. Osmosis must take place as contact is made. Emotions and ideas need to seep back and forth to have a true engagement.

Boundaries that are too rigid will be like the turtle that will not stick its head out of the shell. The inner life is hidden by a fortress, which blocks the entry of other people into its unique state of mind. On the other hand, if the turtle lost its shell and had no boundaries, it would not be recognizable. It would also be defenseless against predators. It would lose its identity and its life. *Boundaries then can give you identity and give you life.*

The United States would become chaotic if the states lost their boundaries. States would lose their identity if they merged into each other, and we did not know where one began and ended. It would not be recognizable, and its unique identity would die.

States then need boundaries for identity, but they also need permeability for connection with other states and the federal government. States could not be all that they could be without this connection. You could not become all you would be without a linkage. You need to have a link. Then, when opportunities come your way, you will not blink. You will become clearheaded and will wisely think. Then you will be the one that can wink.

Boundaries give identity, and we grow by having a welcome sign that invites others into our world. Each state and most towns have a welcome sign as an invitation to enter their unique state. The states are better-off with it. No person needs to be like an island. They will feel like a castaway in a faraway land. Having a welcome mat signals to others that they can get to know us. They know that inquiring about our lives will not create a fuss.

The following questions will always be raised: How autonomous should the states be and remain at optimal health? How dependent should they be upon the federal government? In a friendship or a marriage, how much space and autonomy is needed? How much connection and independence should there be for optimal health?

The turfs or boundaries of workers in the workplace give definition to the job. There is a job description. If the turfs or boundaries are too rigid, they will keep teamwork from creating synergy. Ideas flowing from the top to the bottom as well as from the bottom to the top create optimal health for companies. Employees will give each other creative company.

You are created for uniqueness and for relationships. This uniqueness goes for naught if boundaries are too rigid. The uniqueness is lost if the boundaries are too weak. You need boundaries to know who you are. You need connection with others to maximize your potential. Then you will have the courage and wisdom to make necessary changes in your boundaries to make them healthier. *You will be bound for your promised land!*

Wisdom

A person has wise boundaries when they provide protection.
A person has wise boundaries when they have room for a healthy connection.

Courage

A person has courageous boundaries when a *no* means no,
And a person can draw a line in the sand and keep their dignity in tow.

Serenity

A person remains serene when they can keep people away,
Who, without a boundary, would take advantage of their stay.

The following guiding questions are adapted to the chapter on boundaries. These thought-provoking questions are to help you ponder personal applications and implications of the Serenity Prayer. The resulting soul-searching exercise can aid you to more fully experience the Serenity Prayer lifestyle as you apply this prayer to all aspects of your daily life.

These questions embodied in the Serenity Prayer can then begin a personal lifelong quest in becoming more skillful in living the Serenity Prayer lifestyle. Then the Serenity Prayer can become increasingly embedded in your life. The prayer can help smooth out the edges of life and prevent your lifestyle from becoming coarse. The voice of your life will not become hoarse. The Serenity Prayer then is a great spiritual resource to help you keep the course.

Coaching Questions: Applying the Serenity Prayer to Healthy Boundaries

Remember:

You are not starting from scratch. You have long since been hatched. In your life, your efforts have not gone for naught. You can be commended for what you have already wrought.

These questions and thoughts are for the purpose of serving as a personal coach. They can give you the opportunity to prayerfully surface solutions to your particular situation. You may find an opportunity to build upon what you are already doing well and take another step forward. Engaging the Serenity Prayer with the issue of boundaries can become a profitable soul-searching pilgrimage.

1. **What do you need to accept that you cannot change regarding boundaries?**

"Lord, help me to accept the things that I cannot change regarding the issues on the boundaries of people in the past and present."

It is very difficult to let go of the unalterable aspects of life. They can bring us to the altar when we falter in reducing our internal strife. For example, if someone in the past has intruded upon your boundary, you cannot change that. Forgive and gradually let go. If you have intruded upon someone else's boundary, forgive yourself, learn, and gradually let go. Also, you may not like the boundaries of your significant others, but they may not be changeable.

2. **What do you need to change that are changeable regarding boundaries?**

We can make a difference that counts. And the worthless behaviors we will renounce. One may need to become more assertive and say no when they need to say no. Protecting one's boundaries is important. Building trust can enable one to expand the boundaries of others to include oneself. The boundary has experienced a positive, expanding change.

3. **What are some things you can change that you may be striving to change in the wrong manner regarding boundaries?**

"Lord, help me to stop changing aspects regarding boundaries in the wrong manner."

Does the end justify the means?

Is the process worthy of the progress?

Does the manner of change have good manners?

It can help by thinking of an example of what you have changed in a good manner. Begin from a positive feeling.

When one changes things in the wrong way, there is no serenity.

There will likely only be enmity. For example, one may be striving to change to be more assertive, but one is becoming too aggressive.

4. What are you striving to change that you should not be trying to change regarding boundaries?

"Lord, help me to stop striving to change boundaries that I should leave alone." To be nosy can become very noisy. For example, one may strive to intrude upon another's boundary to change them. One needs to give others their private space.

Trying to make improvements may be in the best of intentions, but these efforts can result in futile dissensions. For example, one may feel that the dog and the cat should have the same boundaries. One must stop striving to make everybody's boundaries the same. Just because they are different does not mean that they need to be fixed.

5. What are some aspects regarding boundaries that you do not know if they are changeable or not changeable?

"Lord, help me to decide if I should strive to change an aspect of boundaries or let it go."

There are times when the decision is not clear whether something can be changed that is so dear. This takes a time of prayer and a time to explore to help make the decision that one will not deplore. For example, can one build trust and find a gate to open. One may find that the person needs private space but can benefit from some connection. You may be that sensitive connection that reaches out but does not force its way in.

6. How can serenity, wisdom, and courage help you to become more empowered to fashion healthy boundaries?

"Lord, help me to utilize the powerful dynamics of serenity, wisdom, and courage to have healthy boundaries." The Serenity Prayer gives us meaning and purpose and helps us to live life filled with an overflowing surplus.

Imagine what you would look, feel, and act like if you were filled with *wisdom* regarding boundaries.

Visualize what you would look, feel, and act like if you were filled with *courage* regarding boundaries.

Envision what you would look, feel, and act like if you were filled with *serenity* regarding boundaries.

In each state, how would your body language appear?

What would be your facial expression?

How would you look out of your eyes?

What would the tone of your voice sound like?

What more would you be accomplishing?

How would you envision others responding to you differently?

How would you project your life to be different today, in one week, in one month, in one year, in five years . . . ? Your life would be different indeed.

Cultivate these feelings. Get a vision, and it will turn into a mission—a mission statement that is empowered. You can apply a vision and a mission to the vast array of your present and future challenges. The Serenity Prayer can serve as fission to spark the energy to carry out the plan.

7. What do I need to change behaviorally concerning boundaries?

"Lord, help me to change what I should change regarding my behaviors concerning boundaries?"

You need to affirm what you are doing well. Owning these strengths can help you feel swell. You can then take the next step with inspiration. Then the next step of growth will not be out of desperation. One can begin to row with the flow and experience life's progressive journey with a glow. For example, one may need to give their partner more space.

8. What do I need to change regarding my attitude concerning boundaries?

"Lord, help me to change my feelings and attitudes regarding boundaries that I need to change."

One's attitude is one's life's outlook. If it is negative, it can lead to a donnybrook. If it is positive, it can provide one a life's stance to celebrate each day with the attitude of wanting to dance. For example, one may need to let go of the feeling that one needs to know all the private thoughts of their mate. Everyone needs some private space. Also, one's boundaries may be too rigid because of a defensive attitude. One needs to be less defensive and become more open. Then the next step is to become healthier on the offensive without becoming offensive.

Chapter 10

Responding to Difficult People with Serenity

Difficult people are here to stay.
We will do well to find a coping way.

The Serenity Prayer as a coach can help you to cope.
Positive responses can prevent you from wanting to mope.

The difficult person wants to be top dog.

The Serenity Prayer raises these issues regarding relating to difficult people. You need to know what to strive to change, how to change what you should change, what not to attempt to change, and what is unchangeable. Growing in understanding these tasks as they relate to dealing with thorny people takes serenity, wisdom, and courage.

Therefore, engaging the Serenity Prayer with the issue of responding to difficult people can become a profitable soul-searching pilgrimage. The questions at the end of the chapter can help you to ponder and personally apply the issues that this chapter raises. In the process, you will be honing skills that will enable you to apply the prayer to all aspects of your life.

The Serenity Prayer obviously applies to dealing with difficult people. Thorny people are all about control. A sly person is often over controlling or, in some disheartening manner, striving to knock one's balance off to gain control. The obnoxious person may try to derail a person's feeling of empowerment by continually railing. Having the Serenity Prayer as a mentor and coach can prevent one from failing.

Winning by intimidation or by some intrusive uncomfortable method may be his/her style. Changing what one can and accepting what one cannot change with serenity is at the core of coping with devious people. We cannot change difficult people. We can only change our reaction to them. Having the skill to know whether to respond to difficult people or how to respond can help promote serenity within ourselves. We can deal with difficult people and stay centered if we have been properly mentored.

Years ago, I had a neighbor with a high-shrill barking dog. He would bark for hours. After a hard day's work, coming home to the sound of this piercing barking rattled my bones. After weeks of tolerating this relentlessly piercing barking, I approached the neighbor when she was outside. She said she was tired of the barking as well and would solve the problem. The next day this chronic barking still sent harsh vibrations in the air. The signals that they transmitted were filled with disrupting static. This revolting experience was quite dramatic.

Several attempts were made to try to solve the problem. I went for outside help. The dog shelter came by, and the owner quickly took the dog inside. Being interviewed by the shelter employee was to no avail. The neighbor's remarks led the dog shelter staff to believe that it was my problem.

The police were called. The neighbor took the dog inside. The policeman said, "You have a good story, but her story is better."

Then a few days later, I called the police and had a neighbor as a witness as he had problems with this person as well. Not only did the policeman believe the witness, but he also went outside and caught the lady in the act of trying to hide the dog. He told her she had to get him a collar that would give him a mild shock when he barked. I thought the problem had been solved, but the lady did not put the collar on the dog.

The police said I could take her to court. At best, the court would fine her $200 and then she would not change her behavior and the dog would be left to begin barking again. It did not appear that taking the time-out for court would be worth the effort.

To cope with the situation, I began to sing as the dog barked. It was a lark or a frivolous time that helped me to transcend the previous nerve-racking experience. We certainly did not sound like the music of the melodious lark, but my life became more harmonious and melodious in relationship to this difficult person who would not amend the difficult situation.

Even though we did not become amenable, the animosity stopped. What seemed atrocious and circumstantially odious seemed more melodious. It created harmony and peace within, and freedom from being captivated by the unchangeable situation began. Embarking upon a new attitude rendered the barking to an experience that elicited gratitude even though this difficult person's behavior became rude. She reduced her obnoxious behavior as it lost its power to produce a sour flavor. I found the Serenity Prayer in helping me to accept what I could not change, an invaluable savior. I meant could

We bark, bark, bark all day long.
This barking keeps our lungs strong.
The sound of the barking rises in the air,
As an expression to God of two souls in prayer.

I made about twenty rhyming verses of which the above lines comprised the chorus. It was my way to have some fun regarding a situation in which I had no control. The lady later talked over the fence and said that the prayer had touched her. Her behavior still did not change. "Lord, help me to accept the things that I cannot change." My attitude changed by not taking the situation so seriously by gaining a sense of humor.

To have a sense of control, you need to feel a sense of centeredness that results in a feeling of being balanced. An athlete takes an athletic stance to create as much power in his sport as possible. The opposition will strive to get the athlete off balanced. Dealing with difficult people can result in becoming imbalanced. You can lose your athletic mental stance and consequently lose your effectiveness.

We may wish that we did not have to come in contact with obnoxious people. In reality, people have been striving to make other people miserable for thousands of years. As we expand our lives' horizons, we increase the risk of rubbing shoulders with people who may rub us the wrong way.

Difficult people can dilute our effectiveness in the workplace and in every aspect of life. Our reactions to people who are troublesome can be the pivotal point. We can allow them to diminish us as a people, or we can become demonstrably larger in dealing with this pervasive challenge.

We need to respond in such a fashion that will prevent difficult people from sapping our energies. Our athletic mental agility needs to be kept. Staying centered is needed to hit the bull's-eye regarding dealing effectively with people who bully. Then, we can succeed in this challenging arena of life. Thorny people are striving to gain more leverage. They may drive people to engage in their favorite beverage. Instead of allowing them to drive one to drink, one needs to find a way to develop an equal link. Then we will not feel thorns that can create many woes. We may find out that this thorny person contains a budding rose.

People who are troublesome are troubled, and they either act in their pain or act it out. It is the people who act out their inner pain that creates suffering for those around them. It is important for us not to be a shock absorber for their pain.

Water does run off a duck's back. The Serenity Prayer can back us up and give us the backbone to influence difficult people to back down. Our backs will not be backed up against the Wailing Wall. We will not have to buckle under the unnecessary load. The difficult person's behavior will not become debilitating. As we duck, we will not be stuck with the difficult person's behavior. Like the ducks, we can stay afloat. We can find a way not to let them unduly affect our lives as we develop the skill to avoid their negative vibes.

The word *coping* means to contend on equal terms. The goal of coping is to utilize behaviors that balance the power and minimize the difficulty of the encounter. This skill can prevent the impact from knocking the breath out of us emotionally.

When I was in the sixth grade, I went out for football. I weighed one hundred pounds. It was a small school in a small town. The popular guys were the ones who played football. I wanted to be a part of this group. We were taught how to tackle in the initial stages of practice. One by one, we were to tackle a person coming directly toward us. The fundamentals of tackling were to be demonstrated.

It came my turn to tackle. The person who was coming toward me was an eighth grader who was solid muscle weighing 150 pounds. As we collided, I tackled him with the correct fundamentals. Then he got up and I did not. Tackling this person completely knocked the breath out of me as his knee powered into my fragile stomach. I could barely breathe.

The coach came over and loosened my belt. He pulled me up and down by the waist until I began to breathe more normally. We may feel like we have had the breath knocked out of us emotionally if we do not have the coping skills to deal with a difficult person.

I could not cope with this sport. I changed what I could change and joined the golf team.

When someone is a pain, we can use this opportunity as growing pains. A bottle of hot sauce states, "It hurts so good." Dealing with difficult people can hurt so good and become a spice of life instead of being a slice off our well-being.

Dealing with Difficult People: Understanding the Enemy

Difficult people are miserable inside. They often deal with their misery by casting their gallstones and kidney stones on those by their side. Coping with the challenging behavior of another depends upon understanding ourselves as well as the other.

When you become more insightful about who you are, you are better prepared to develop skills to counter the culprit. When the culprit is yourself, you may become more of the problem than the person you are encountering. At a minimum, you will be less skillful in handling the problem. Two difficult people dealing with each other may result in an escalating, reactive, toxic encounter. The poisonous effects will have no antidote as each person strives to put venom in the cup of the other person's life.

To begin to deal with difficult people then, you must start with yourself. You need to become your own best friend. You might take this vow: "I take myself to be my own best friend to love and to cherish for the rest of my life." This kind of attitude can prevent you from much strife.

A healthy dose of self-esteem can relieve the difficulty you have with yourself. You can become your own worst enemy. You can create enmity. When you are hard on yourself, you can have more difficulty in dealing with people who are hard on you. Then you will not have the foundation to demand respect from others who are not after your own well-being. You can contribute to your difficulty with people. The Serenity Prayer as a coach can bring help from the steeple. We are unfinished pieces of work that can stand in the way of dealing with another person's quirk. A dose of self-esteem is the doctor's orders to lessen our sensitivity. Then we can have the foundation not to overreact to another's negativity.

The difficult person may go for the jugular and tear into our vulnerable psyche, producing a tear in one's eyes. You may become rattled and seem like a rattler instead of a friend to one's self. This is a challenge to overcome, especially if you have had long repetitive, negative responses from difficult people as a child.

The person may know your vulnerabilities. With this insight, the devious person can become a detriment to your self-esteem. You may be susceptible to surrendering your power. As a result, you may take a victim's stance. You may feel like a prisoner as you feel emotionally captured by the bully. The reprehensible, offensive behavior may result in you feeling like you are held in captivity. You can be prayerfully coached to become on the offensive.

To offset the person by reproach, you can be patient with yourself as you create a sturdy fortress preventing the stones from hitting your heart. People will not likely continue to become difficult to you when you have a high level of self-esteem. This strength will help you not to succumb to the bully's mischievous ploys. They will not be able to become detriments to your experiencing life's joys.

Having painful, underlying feelings can also create a challenge in dealing with difficult people. You may magnify the slightest provocation that could seem like a foreboding mountain too steep to climb. An overreaction resulting from your triggered torment could create an avalanche. Your inner pain can create unwise reactionary jaunts in reaction to a difficult person's intentional, revolting taunts.

A high self-esteem can provide the basis to allow slights to run off your backs. These put-downs will then not create a blip on the screen of your psychological map. With a low self-esteem, the radar may be too sensitive. The radar may pick up signals that are misinterpreted as enemies when enemies are not there. If the enemy does exist, you may magnify the difficulty of the person. As a result, your response may be an overreaction, either acting out or acting in your feelings. Dealing with difficult people then begins with looking at the deficiencies within yourself. Then you will have taken the Serenity Prayer off the shelf.

When a difficult person tries to knock you off balance, you can stay in steady by keeping your self-esteem intact. You can take the bull out of the bully and understand what they say as a bunch of bulls. You will be free to go on to the next task because the emotional aftereffects of the encounters with difficult people will not last. Then you will be able to experience life as a challenging blast.

Not only do you need to understand yourself, but you also need to know what makes a difficult person tick. This understanding can prevent them from being like a tick, sticking on you and sucking the joy of life out of you.

Difficult people often wear a chip on their shoulders. As a result, they often chip away at the happiness of others. They are hanging on to the past. They feel victimized. Having a lack of empowerment, they resort to manipulation and provocation to gain what they want. Because they have been tormented by someone in the past, they bedevil others in the present. They may be like bedbugs that bug us during the day.

They have not come to terms with their personal history. Throwing others off balance helps them to feel more stability. Being difficult is not the result of having a bad day. It is their response to having a bad life. People who are difficult may have experienced a tragedy. You cannot cure them, but you can cope with a wise strategy. One strategy is not to allow them to get our goat. You will then not become reactive and be able to cope. You can stay in control by being serene, courageous, and wise. Then you will not experience a tragic demise.

Other difficult people may feel entitled because of a background where they have no one to give them a sense of responsibility and accountability. They have been used to being given things without exerting a sense of effort. Thus, some people become cantankerous because they are greedy. Dealing with difficult people can be unnerving. They can cause the car of our lives to begin swerving. As you understand that they are operating out of a sense that life owes them a debt, you can deal with them by becoming more adept.

Possessions may be more important than people. To obtain what they want, they use people. They are not team players. The rules of fair play are not utilized. Their aggressive behavior is insensitive to the consequences they create in the lives of people they encounter. They are only interested in how others can be used to meet their own self-centered needs.

Some people are difficult because they have a substance abuse problem or a mental illness or both. These people can become very difficult to deal with because they may be in denial. It may be difficult to make a deal with them at the present time. You do not need to take other people's problems as your own, or you will gradually feel a sharpening pain that will cut to the bone. There may be some way you can offer them help without feeling like you have to do it alone.

Some people may become temporarily difficult because they are sick or tired. This is not pervasive behavior. They are having a bad day as a result of being temporarily stressed-out. Their minds, bodies, and spirits are momentarily overloaded. When they become rested and centered, the reactive, difficult behavior will no longer be the center of attention.

In extreme cases, people are malicious, evil, and dangerous. They are frighteningly destructive in their behavior. Encountering a person of this nature may require police protection. They need external controls such as a jail to keep them in check. There are no inner reins. They have to be reined in.

Understanding difficult people can help you maintain some objectivity and rational thought. Then you are able to keep proper emotional distance by not taking the difficult people's reactions personally. You may realize that the behavior is a pervasive problem in the person's life. Many people besides us have been the brunt of the person's scheming actions. Not feeling the brunt of their behavior can prevent you from feeling like a runt. Difficult people can often be understood. This understanding can keep you out of the woods. You can stay in the bright sun's rays to help you have happier days.

Focused confrontation can diffuse difficult people. I remember when I was a pastor, I gathered people around me who consented to being on a steering committee to work on organizing a volunteer chaplaincy program in a hospital. These volunteers were to minister to people who had no pastor or who were in crisis situations. Another role involved being a liaison to the pastor of a person in the hospital.

In the first meeting to begin organizing the volunteer group, one of the ministers said, "You will never get busy ministers to join you in this venture." I then responded by saying, "You consented to being on this committee. Why have you decided not to support its mission?" From that time forward, he did not stand in the way of the effort, which became a resounding success.

Sometimes the response can be a positive stroke. When I was a student at the seminary, I substituted teaching in the inner-city schools in a very difficult time. On one occasion, I turned around from writing on the blackboard to find the students in a circle, with two students face-to-face with each other, ready to fight. The other students had picked up their desks and formed a circle around the students.

I went up to them, and one student said, "Teacher, you take your glasses off. I am going to beat your head in." I told him that I bet he could beat me up if he wanted to. He said, "Yes, I could." Then he went back to his seat and sat down.

A stroke to his ego had stabilized a difficult situation. It was a positive leverage that brought calmness to the classroom setting. He no longer had any reason to prove anything to his peers. Of course, this way of dealing with a similar situation may not work with all people. It may take another approach.

Here are some other examples of what to say in more normal circumstances when people are angry. "Have you tried . . ." "Let's talk about this for a minute."

An angry person wants to be heard and respected. Listen to an angry person. Don't try to calm him. Listening can calm a difficult person's anger. Give the person the opportunity to vent their anger. Don't trivialize it, but don't over validate it either. "I can see that you're angry." Recognizing their anger and letting it flow may reduce its intensity. Then reason in communication may prevail, and one may open up an opportunity to problem solve instead of increasing the person's tendency to rail.

Developing a repertoire of behaviors can be the leverage to equalize the power. You can gain the foundation to develop behaviors to best respond to people who have the motivation to rob you of our good day. Your skillful responses can keep them at bay.

Forgiveness: A Wise Choice in Responding to Thorny People

Forgiveness can be a healing response to difficult people. Effectively dealing with difficult people may require a forgiving spirit. Letting go of one's bitterness and the feeling of wanting revenge may be the most difficult task of all. A difficult person's behavior can sometimes leave a gash. This infected wound will not quickly dash. Forgiveness can feel insurmountable to begin, but it can be a process of healing within.

If someone shot and killed your loved one, you would not say immediately, "I forgive you. You must have had a bad day." It is similar to a grief process. You have to go through stages in order to come to terms with the damage of the underserved trauma. Otherwise, it would be premature forgiveness.

You must allow yourself to feel the impact of the injustice and work through the hurt and anger. If you do not, at least allow yourself to begin the journey of healing. The negative impact of the event can become unyielding. Forgiveness is not for the fainthearted, but it may help keep you from fainting. To forgive another person should not be a simple matter. It is a process of working through a mixture of feelings that sits on your platter. If you partake of the emotional poison, it can eat you alive. One's life then can take a nosedive. One can gradually reduce what is on one's plate. This reduction can begin to ease the almost unbearable heartache. Then this impact will no longer significantly affect your life. Instead of taking a nosedive, your life will begin to become more alive.

Forgiveness has to come when it is time. The time is never perfect. At some point, one needs to make the decision to forgive and begin to come to terms with the injustice that they did not deserve. It is not always wise to talk directly with the devious person. A face-to-face connection could make the wound worsen. One forgives to heal one's own anger. It can be done between oneself and God to diminish the rancor.

One may not completely recover from such a trauma. Complete forgiveness may not be obtained, but it can begin a journey of healing that can be maintained. A soul that has been wrenched by the unmerciful trauma can find rest by gradually granting pardon. A wrenched soul can become a wasteland, barren and bare. This rancor can keep you locked in an emotionally intense stare. Forgiveness can bring back life's flavor. This wise act can result in doing yourself a colossal favor.

The enormity of the difficulty of forgiveness can be overcome. The fruits of one's labor can be harvested. As one begins the harvesting process, it is important that one realizes that forgiveness gets one off the hook, but not the perpetrator. What this person does in the sanctuary of their souls is their responsibility.

None of us are professional forgivers. We need to take the leap and start the process toward getting the feelings behind us. Sunlight can break through the cloud of cynicism. The chip on a difficult person's shoulder will no longer chip away at our fulfillment in life. We will be able to accept what we cannot change. We will become a chip off the Serenity Prayer's God-given block. Your life will no longer be in a negative, emotional lock. You will be free to live with God's love in full stock.

Wisdom

It takes wisdom to cope constructively with difficult people's behavior. We have to accept that we cannot be their saviors. We can stand up and be counted as one who did not allow their behaviors to result in our feeling discounted.

Courage

It takes courage to cope with a person with a devious way. We need to know when to retreat and when to step in the fray. Our response can light the fuse or defuse the person with a mal heart. We can level the playing field by letting them know that we will not fall apart. As we stay centered and steady, the intruder will leave because he is ready.

Serenity

It takes serenity to stay calm and not overreact when we are under attack. Serenity can calm the situation and result in a quick, quieting persuasion.

The following guiding questions are adapted to the chapter on difficult people. These thought-provoking questions are to help you ponder personal applications of the Serenity Prayer. The resulting soul-searching exercise can aid you to more fully experience the Serenity Prayer lifestyle as you apply this prayer to all aspects of your daily life.

These questions embodied in the Serenity Prayer then can begin a personal lifelong quest in becoming more skillful in living the Serenity Prayer lifestyle. Then the Serenity Prayer can become increasingly embedded in your life. The prayer can help smooth out the edges of life and prevent your lifestyle from becoming coarse. The voice of your life will not become hoarse. The Serenity Prayer then is a great spiritual resource to help you keep the course.

Coaching Questions: The Serenity Prayers Informs Coping with Difficult People

Remember:

You are not starting from scratch. You have long since been hatched. Your efforts have not gone for naught. You can be commended for what you have already wrought.

These questions and thoughts are for the purpose of serving as personal coaches. They can give you the opportunity to prayerfully brainstorm to surface the challenges and solutions in your particular situation.

You may find an opportunity to build upon what you are already doing well and take another step forward. Engaging the Serenity Prayer with the issue of responding to difficult people can become a profitable soul-searching pilgrimage.

1. **What do you need to accept that you cannot change regarding dealing with difficult people?**

"Lord, help me to accept what I cannot change regarding the issue of dealing with shrewd people."

It is very difficult to let go of the unalterable aspects of life. You can come to the altar when you falter in reducing your internal strife. You may have a difficult boss, coworker, neighbor, etc., that you cannot change.

2. **What do you need to change that are changeable regarding the matter of relating to scheming people?**

"Lord, grant me the serenity, wisdom, and courage that I need to change what I can regarding relating to difficult people."

You can make a difference that counts, and the worthless behaviors you will renounce.

3. **What are some things you can change that you may be striving to change in the wrong manner regarding relating to conniving people?**

"Lord, help me to have the serenity, wisdom, and courage to stop trying to relate to devious people in the wrong manner."

Does the end justify the means?

Is the process worthy of the progress?

Does the manner of change have good manners?

It can help by thinking of an example of what you have changed in a good manner. Begin with a positive feeling.

When you make changes in the wrong way, there is no serenity. There will likely only be enmity. You may try to retaliate in a relationship with a difficult person. Retaliating with a thorny person may result in the problem escalating. You may diffuse the anger by staying centered and by not allowing the difficult person to get the upper hand. It is imperative to avoid a power struggle.

4. **What are you striving to change regarding difficult people that you should not be trying to change?**

"Lord, help me to stop trying to change the things about thorny people that I should not strive to change."
Trying to make improvements may be in the best of intentions, but these efforts can result in futile dissensions. For example, you may be trying too hard to make the relationship work with a difficult person.

5. **What are some things that you do not know whether they are changeable or not changeable regarding difficult people?**

"Lord, give me the wisdom to know whether it is possible to strive to change myself in a relationship with a person that is devious."
There are times when the decision is not clear whether something can be changed that is so dear. This takes a time of prayer and a time to explore to grant one an opportunity to make the decision that one will not deplore. Often these answers are not easy, but one needs to search in a wise manner. It may be a difficult environment of people at work, etc.

6. **How can the powerful dynamics of serenity, wisdom, and courage help you deal more effectively with difficult people?**

"Lord, grant me the guidance to fully utilize serenity, wisdom, and courage to relate to difficult people in a sound manner."

The Serenity Prayer gives us meaning and purpose
And helps us to live life filled with an overflowing surplus.

Imagine what you would look, feel, and act like if you were filled with wisdom in dealing with difficult people.

Envision what you would look, feel, and act like if you were filled with courage in dealing with difficult people.

Visualize what you would look, feel, and act like if you were filled with serenity in dealing with difficult people.

With each trait regarding dealing with difficult people, how would your body language appear?

What would be your facial expression?

How would you look out of your eyes?

What would the tone of your voice sound like?

What more would you be accomplishing?

How would you envision people responding differently to you?

How would you project your life to be different today, in one week, in one month, in one year, in five years . . . ? Your life would be different indeed.

Cultivate these feelings. Develop a vision, and it will turn into a mission—a mission statement that is empowered. You can apply a vision and a mission to the vast array of your present and future challenges. The Serenity Prayer can serve as fission to spark the energy to carry out the plan.

7. **What do you need to change behaviorally in relating to difficult people?**

"Lord, grant me the wisdom to know what I need to change in my conduct regarding dealing with difficult people."

> You need to affirm what you are doing well.
> Owning these strengths can help you feel swell.
>
> You can then take the next step with inspiration.
> Then the next step of growth will not be out of desperation.
>
> One can begin to row with the flow
> And experience life's progressive journey with a glow.
>
> Changing one's actions relating to a difficult person may make
>   for smoother sailing.
> Then one can keep from experiencing anguish that results in
>   railing.

8. **What do you need to change regarding your attitude in relating to difficult people?**

"Lord, grant me the wisdom, serenity, and courage to change my attitudes and feelings that I need to alter regarding relating to difficult people."

One's attitude is one's life's outlook. If it is negative, it can lead to a donnybrook. If it is positive, it can provide one a life's stance to celebrate each day with the attitude of wanting to dance. For example, one may feel that they should be able to have a positive relationship with anyone, and that ability is not realistic.

Chapter 11

Networking: Changing What You Thought You Could Not Change

By networking we can uncover talents that were previously untapped.
A support system can keep these talents from being zapped.

The Serenity Prayer raises these issues regarding changing circumstances that we thought were unchangeable. One needs to know what to strive to change, how to change what one should change, what not to attempt to change what one cannot change. Growing in accomplishing these tasks regarding tapping our latent potential certainly takes serenity, wisdom, and courage.

Engaging the Serenity Prayer with the issue of discovering more of our potential can become a profitable soul-searching pilgrimage. The questions at the end of the chapter help one to ponder and apply the issues that this chapter raises in one's personal situation.

It is fitting that networking is the final chapter. We need to have a support system to be the best that we can be. A support system can unlock more of our potential. Bouncing ideas off other trusted people can be an enlightening and strengthening process. I have changed portions of this book with suggestions. Networking has enhanced my talents.

When we have people believing in us and counting on us, we can be inspired to change what we previously thought we could not change. Operating in a vacuum could become like a vacuum cleaner sucking out one's talents that could be tapped. The potential of one could be left untapped. Without having a supportive network, the naysayers can be demeaning, and our talents may be zapped. Sometimes we do not know that we can accomplish. It may be that someone has decided to admonish. Our doubts about ourselves then may increase. Then how we feel about our abilities may decrease.

A support system can give our efforts momentum, keeping them streaming. A stream is always flowing and moving. A supportive network can become a vital part of our stream to keep us flowing forward toward our destination. Then streaming can give us meaning and prevent us from screaming.

Learning what we can change sometimes takes trial and error. Sometimes it is keeping on keep on until a breakthrough comes. This exploration is vital. The secret is when to know to let it go—sports, science, politics, acting, etc. Learning when to draw the line can keep our efforts in line. We can learn from our failures and use them in our next ventures. Sometimes the only way to know if you can change or accomplish something is to give it a go.

We need people around us that we do not deplore. People who we admire and who respect us may help us explore. Then as we consider what we can change, it will be more. This stimulating environment will be anything but a bore.

We can cultivate a strong belief in ourselves that can overcome obstacles. We will not see what is surmountable as insurmountable. We will gain the wisdom to distinguish between the two. The musical instruments of our lives will be in tune with what is changeable and what is unchangeable. When we are tone death, we do not know when our lives are out of tune of trying to play notes we cannot play.

We need to tune out the false prophets and tune in to the truth. The truth can give us the belief and faith in ourselves that will move mountains. The vistas of life will become more scenic the further we climb. We will ring the chimes of our life's purpose.

When someone says that it cannot be done, it is something to be considered, but it is not necessarily something that could make one reconsider. We must not obsess over what the naysayers say. We may become susceptible to taking a recess that does not hear the bell that says recess is over. We will miss the learning opportunities to conquer our learning curves.

We need to network with God and other people. This is the heart of any recovery program. Churches use this practical truth. AA uses it in its profoundly successful twelve-step program to help people take steps forward in their program.

Any challenge that we encounter will be handled better with a support system. Support is imperative if we are going to be able to change what we can change. As a result, often we can become empowered to accomplish goals that we previously thought were not accomplishable.

All presidents have advisors to help them to be at their best. More and more people are having personal coaches. We may not be able to have a personal coach, but we can use people as mentors. We need to keep growing to master what we can change. We need to keep on growing if we are going to gain the wisdom to distinguish between what we cannot change and what we can.

If we go to it alone, we will miss the boat in what we may change. We will not be open to wise feedback when we are barking up the wrong tree. We need to be careful who we place in our support system. We do not need yes people. But at the same time, we do not need negative people as well. We need wise people to help us to gather information to make the best decisions possible.

We are the executives of our lives. The full responsibility of the decisions that we make is ours. We need to know that "the buck stops here." The bucking bronco will not be as likely to buck us off if we network with others. Clarity can be enhanced, and strength can be gained by our spirituality, knowledge gathering, and networking with others. We may gain a buck.

We can magnify our efforts by looking to others for help. Then we can change what we can without giving a yelp. Our lives are much stronger when we share the task. Without help, we may never last. With help, we may never last. With support our possibilities will be vast.

Sometimes we need outside help to change what we cannot change. When I used the YMCA, I usually used the jogging track and the swimming pool. One occasion I saw a stationary bike when I passed the weight room. Normally, I would have passed it up. This time I decided to use the stationery bike. As I entered the weight room, I saw a person who had been bench-pressing heavy weights. I looked at him, and to my alarm, he was stuck as he had the weights just above his neck.

He was too exhausted to push the weights above him and set them in the rack. He was hanging helplessly on for dear life as he was continuing to lose energy. It would not have been long until exhaustion would set in, and he could no longer hold the bar above his neck. The heavy bar with weights on each side was on the brink of beginning its descent upon his neck.

I went over to him and both of us together raised the bar above him and put it in the slot. He was helpless by himself, but with a little assistance from me, he reached his goal. We can feel helpless by ourselves and feel like we have to accept what we cannot change. But with other people's help, there may be some creative answers to our challenges.

There is a story that has been circulating around that is well worth repeating. A man was on top of his house, and a flood was engulfing his house.

He prayed, "Lord, get me out of this situation."

A helicopter came over and dropped down a ladder. The man was still praying, "Lord, help me get out of here." The helicopter could not wait any longer and went to help others.

Then a boat arrived, and a ladder came out of the boat and stretched to the roof. After a while, the boat had to leave to help others who wanted help.

The man was very angry at God. "Why don't you help me?"

He said, "I sent you a helicopter."

Mountain climbers go in groups. They help each other. They become a team that helps each individual reach the summit.

If we do not connect with others, we can make a mountain out of a molehill. Life will be harder than it has to be. The obstacles will be magnified to proportions that are beyond reality.

There have been virtually no people that have impactful accomplishments without help outside of themselves. Any sports figure will give thanks to many people who help them obtain success. Great artists will report that they were influenced by many other artists that came before them or were their contemporaries. Even Shakespeare was influenced by writers that preceded him. Creativity often does not create something new. Accomplishments are built upon knowledge gained before. If we are not open to be influenced or helped by other people, we may miss the boat.

It may be constructive criticism that becomes the turning point in our accomplishing something that we previously felt impossible. The things that we cannot change may be changeable. We do need the wisdom to know if there is a key that will unlock the door. If there is no key, we need to realize that as one door closes, there is another one that will open.

The "I do it myself" attitude is not always the best formula for success. The people who built a life out West in the days of the frontier were admired for their independent self-sufficiency. Self-sufficiency was needed in that time and place. On the other hand, society grows faster when people and cultures linked together to share information. Cultures stagnated when there was no history to build upon and the knowledge was lost. This isolation led to the Dark Ages.

The age of the Enlightenment was ignited by people linking together to form a chain of events that culminated in the blossoming of knowledge, which improved humankind as a whole. Self-sufficiency is carried too far when we do not look outside ourselves to see how we can improve by rubbing shoulders with others.

> The Panama Canal would have never been built,
> If hundreds of people had not worked to the hilt.

One needs to network and gain a support system. We need both a vertical relationship with God and a horizontal relationship with people. Then the ship of our lives will go through the canal to our destination.

Wisdom

Wisdom helps what can and cannot be changed to become clearer.

> One can discover what one thought was unchangeable and can
> be altered.
> Without networking with other people many have faltered.
> Networking with others can bring one success.
> This can maximize your talents helping you not to have to
> guess.
> Bouncing off ideas from others helps one not to flounder.
> One can gain a pathway to a result that is much sounder.

Courage

Courage can be enhanced by others cheering you on.

Their belief in you can empower you to spawn creative ideas.
The momentum that you receive can zap your fears. You will see
your goals as adventures as your networking has become a
powerful virtue.

Serenity

Serenity can attract others around you. Your calm manner can make
others be true. Your way with people will be soothing and efficient. You will
find you can do things that you previously felt deficient.

Coaching Questions: The Serenity Prayer and Networking

Remember:

You are not starting from scratch. You have long since been hatched.
Your efforts have not gone for naught. You can be commended for what
you have already wrought.

You may find an opportunity to build upon what you are already
doing well and take another step forward. Engaging the Serenity Prayer
with the issue of networking can become a profitable soul-searching
pilgrimage.

**How can serenity, wisdom, and courage help me in the issue of being
able to change what I previously thought was unchangeable?**

"Lord, give me the guidance to use the powerful, dynamic traits of
wisdom, courage, and serenity to help me in the issue of being able to change
what I previously thought I could not change."

*The Serenity Prayer gives us meaning and purpose
And helps us to live life filled with a surplus.*

Imagine what you would look, feel, and act like if you were filled with
wisdom to change what you previously thought you could not change.

Visualize what you would look, feel, and act like if you were filled with
courage to change what you previously thought you could not change.

Envision what you would look, feel, and act like if you were filled with
serenity to change what you previously thought you could not change.

Having each trait, how would your body language look?

What would be your facial expression?

How would you look out of your eyes?

What would the tone of your voice sound like?

What more would you be accomplishing?

How would you project your life to be different today, in one week, in one month, in one year, in five years . . . ? Your life would be different indeed.

Cultivate these feelings. Get a vision, and it will turn into a mission—a mission statement that is empowered. The Serenity Prayer can serve as a catalyst to spark the energy to carry out your plans.

Author's Note

If there are one or two changes that you make regarding applying the Serenity Prayer to your life, then this book would have been worth it. Small changes can be huge in their impact. They can become seeds that blossom into a beautiful bouquet. It is important not to become imprisoned in perfectionism. This book would be misinterpreted if it puts you on a guilt trip because you feel that you are not serene enough. Accept where you are and recognize that small changes are vital. How do you eat an elephant? You eat it one bite at a time.

No one is serene all the time. When you become upset, you do have many resources. The Serenity Prayer is a valuable resource in helping you to become centered when you are frazzled. You may be like a sheep that has gone astray, but you can be gently brought back to the serene presence of the shepherd. An uncontrollable circumstance may knock the breath out of you. The Serenity Prayer can help breathe within you the breath of life.

This book should not be read and then left to collect dust on the shelf. It can become a resource to enable positive life changes on your quest. These changes can grant you a growing sense of zest.

It is to be used as a resource to serve as reminders regarding applying the prayer to our lives. By faithfully incorporating this prayer into daily living, it can eventually become a natural habit.

To make it work, you will not have to be like a magician pulling a rabbit out of a hat. By prayerfully utilizing this prayer, a more positive lifestyle can result. May this amazing prayer grant you an abundance of serenity. You deserve amazing grace for a graceful living that will last for an eternity.

To a more serene life,

Dan C. Crenshaw

Remember:

God, give us grace to accept with serenity the things that cannot be changed, courage to change the things that should be changed, and the wisdom to distinguish the one from the other.

—Elisabeth Sifton, *The Serenity Prayer:*
Faith and Politics in Times of Peace and War